The Spiritual Life

A Series of Lectures Delivered Before the Students
of the Moody Bible Institute, Chicago in 1895

Revised Edition

Contents

The Work of the Holy Spirit

The Work of Jesus Christ

Preface to the Revised Edition

The aim of this Revised Edition is to make this powerful work more accessible to contemporary readers. The text is largely the same as that of the 1895 First Edition but many editorial revisions have been made to aid clarity:

Typos from the First Edition have been corrected.

Paragraph breaks have been added and other grammatical changes made to aid the flow of the text.

Headings and numbers have been added where Rev. Murray works through a series of points.

Footnotes have been added for easy reference to the many passages of Scripture as well as hymns and other works quoted in the text.

Perhaps most significantly, the order of Chapters 13 and 14 has been reversed. It is clear from the text that the lecture entitled 'Yield Yourselves unto God' was given before 'Willing and Doing'. In fact, 'Willing and Doing' refers to matters discussed in 'Yield Yourselves unto God', so the order in the First Edition was most likely an error.

Imperfections remain, no doubt, but let the message of the Gospel herein transcend the limitations of the editor and even the speaker.

—Chris Juby
(2019)

Preface to the First Edition

Rev. Andrew Murray's writings have been much blessed to thousands in this and other lands; when he came to America, in the summer of 1895, earnest prayers were going up from many hearts that his platform utterances might be even more abundantly blessed. God heard and answered, and the heart and lips of His humble servant were wonderfully touched with the divine fire.

It was our privilege to listen to the Chicago lectures, and to gather stenographic reports for publication, with a view to passing the "spoken word" to many who were deprived of the privilege of listening to this man of God.

We send these printed pages forth, the most of which have been personally revised by Mr. Murray, with a prayer that God may use them to His glory in bringing blessing to many hearts.

—The Publishers
(1895)

1. Carnal or Spiritual
(1 Corinthians 3:1-4)

Throughout the church of Christ there is a universal complaint of the feebleness of the Christian life, and there are tens of thousands of souls longing to know how to lead a better life. They find in God's word promises of perfect peace, of a faith that overcomes the world, of a joy that is unspeakable, of a life of ever abiding communion with Christ, hidden in the hollow of God's hand, and in the secret of his pavilion. But alas, thousands say they know not how to obtain it. Our meetings have just this one object: to try and find out what are the possibilities of the Christian life as God has revealed them in His word, what are the hindrances that keep the majority of believers out of that life, and what are the steps by which to come in and take possession.

I want to begin by calling your attention to what is always important at the outset of these conferences. There are two stages in the Christian life: the lower stage under the power of the flesh, and the stage of the true life in the power of the Spirit. Let me direct your attention to a passage in 1 Corinthians 3:1-4.

There you have the first sorted Christians: some are spiritual and some are carnal. And Paul says he finds it of the utmost importance when he teaches people to find out which of the two they are; for if he gave what is food to the spiritual to the carnal it would not do them any good. "I could not speak unto you as unto spiritual, but as unto carnal, even as unto babes in Christ."[1] You are in Christ, you are real Christians, but alas, you are feeble Christians, just like infants. "I have fed you with milk and not with

---

[1] 1 Corinthians 3:1

meat."[2] There are some truths that are just like milk, suitable for carnal Christians; other truths of God's word—deep spiritual truths—are for spiritual people. "For hitherto ye were not able to bear it, neither yet now are ye able for ye are yet carnal."[3] There you have the word "carnal" again. He says plainly, "I want you to know that you are carnal; believers, but carnal believers," "For"— here comes the proof—"For whereas there is among you envying and strife, and divisions, are ye not carnal, and walk as men?"[4] He asks them to answer the question.

The word "carnal" comes from the Latin word meaning "flesh." If you do the works of the flesh this proves you are carnal, you walk as men do, not as children of God do, who lead a heavenly life. "One says I am of Paul, and another, I am of Apollos; are ye not carnal?"[5] For the fourth time you have the word "carnal" and for the second time the very pointed question for them to answer, "Tell me, are ye not carnal?"

By the help of God, I shall speak to you upon these two points: 1. What it is to be not spiritual but carnal. 2. The way from carnal to spiritual.

1. Not spiritual but carnal

"You are not spiritual but carnal," the apostle says. I am desirous that everyone as we go along try himself and answer the question, "Am I still carnal, or am I by the grace of God spiritual?" You know a doctor cannot do you any good unless there is first a thorough diagnosis of the case. He asks a number of questions, examines

---

[2] 1 Corinthians 3:2
[3] 1 Corinthians 3:2-3
[4] 1 Corinthians 3:3
[5] 1 Corinthians 3:4

your lungs and heart, finds out what is wrong and prescribes the needful remedy. Until you find out what is wrong all the preaching of the most heavenly truths will do you no good. People must be brought to the realizing of their carnal state ere the knowledge of the spiritual life can be any real benefit.

Oh God, we pray Thee, reveal the mystery of the Divine truth; the mystery of our own hearts, and the carnal state; the mystery of the Holy Spirit, and the spiritual life. We pray Thee now to come in and teach us. Give us grace to say, "Lord search me, and if I am carnal, oh, discover it today, and open up to me the way into the spiritual life, to live as a spiritual man." God, grant it.

I think if we look carefully at this passage, we shall find four principal marks of the carnal state:

i. It is a state of protracted infancy.

If I had here today a beautiful little child six months old with its chubby hands and feet, you would say "What a perfect child," but if in three years' time we found that the child had not grown an inch we should conclude that something was the matter. If in another three years we again found no growth, we should at once say there is some terrible disease in that child that prevents its growth, for where there is health there is growth.

That is now what Paul says to the Corinthians: "You are young Christians, babes in Christ." At first a Christian may be carnal for he is young and does not know what sin is, but when a man has been a Christian for some time, say after six months, a year or three years, or even ten years, and he does not grow but remains at the same place where he started from as a babe, there is something the matter; there is some terrible disease; that disease is the carnal mind. A Christian when under the power of the flesh is in a state of protracted infancy.

You find it said in the epistle to the Hebrews that when after they had been so long Christians they ought to be teachers, helping others, they still had to be fed with milk and were not able to take the meat of the full grown man. This is a state of protracted infancy and it is the state of the greater part of the Christian church. How many there are who will testify that the best time was the first three months after conversion; and after that they began to go back; they lost their joy and alas, they have never had such joy since then? They have lost their first love. At that time they used to conquer sin, but now it has the mastery.

What are the marks of a babe? One is the babe cannot help himself, he has got to be helped by others. The other, he cannot help anyone else. Look at a baby in a house: you have got to have mother or sister or nurse to take care of him. A little baby needs always to be helped and cared for. That is the way with many Christians. They go to church, to prayer meetings, conferences, and are ever seeking help from others. A little infant six months old cannot help another; so there are Christians who cannot really help others by their spiritual experience. Dear friends let us take this first mark of carnal state, test ourselves, and if there be no healthy growth let us bow before God in shame.

ii. The carnal state is a state of sin and failure; no victory over sin.

Paul writing to the Corinthians says, "There is among you envying, and strife, and divisions." That was the work of the flesh and this was the great reason that he had to write to them the thirteenth chapter, because of their quarrelling. One exalted Paul, another thought Apollos was the more eloquent; another thought that Peter was older than either and better; they were divided into religious parties. They were just squabbling among themselves and got excited, and had strifes, divisions and envy.

In Galatians, fifth chapter, you have envyings, strifes, etc. as the works of the flesh. Do we not find Christians who in some respects have a good measure of the grace of God and yet have never really conquered their temper, and so when another says a sharp thing to them, they give a sharp reply? How many Christians there are who have never learned to love as God wants them to love—to love the unlovable. What is this but that they are yet in the carnal state? In them the flesh has more power than the Spirit. Friends, until we confess with shame, "I am carnal," we will not get into the life of the spiritual man.

May God search us and reveal our true state. Let us say, "what is it that hinders the brightness of my life?" and you will get the answer from God. Two powers are striving for mastery over you: Spirit and flesh; and if the Spirit is not ruling you it is because the flesh is ruling. This is why a man gives way to pride, self-conceit, worldliness, the lust of the eyes, the lust of the flesh, and the pride of life. It is nothing but that he is still in the carnal state.

You know a thing always gets its name from what is its most prominent characteristic. A spiritual man gets his name from the fact that the Spirit triumphs, rules in his life, even though there may still be somewhat of the flesh. You cannot be in intercourse with him without feeling that the Spirit is leading, guiding and controlling. He is called spiritual because spirituality is his chief characteristic. Paul writes to the Corinthians, "Know ye not that ye are the temple of the Holy Ghost that dwelleth in you."[6] There was somewhat of the Spirit in them, but they had allowed the flesh to rule. The question comes to us, as a voice from heaven, "Are ye not carnal?" That worldliness, that unfaithfulness, that neglect of God's word. It is but the mark of one thing you are carnal, you have not given yourself over wholly to live the spiritual life.

iii. The third mark of the carnal state. Along with this carnal state

---

[6] 1 Corinthians 3:16

there may be found a great deal of spiritual gift.

This is a very solemn thought. You know how this is illustrated in the case of the Corinthians. In the first chapter Paul says, "I thank God ... that in everything ye are enriched by him in all utterance and in all knowledge."[7]

There were spiritual gifts among the Corinthians: gifts of prophecy, tongues, and many other gifts most remarkable. Indeed, the gift of tongues was so remarkable that Paul had to check and warn them to be careful in their use of this gift. And yet Paul writes the whole epistle with the one idea, that they were full of quarrelling, pride, selfishness, etc. A man may have a spiritual gift of preaching or be able to speak with power, and yet his private life may be filled with pride until the world says, "We don't believe in that man. Where is his humility?" A man may be an evangelist and lead hundreds to Christ and yet you will hear it said, "How full of self." The world says, "I don't believe in that man he is too full of himself." Can it be that a man who is a powerful man in the service of God can be carnal? It can be. That is what we want to make plain.

A man may claim the baptism of the Holy Spirit and get it as a Spirit of power and a Spirit of zeal, and yet that man may be terribly lacking in the graces of a holy life—in humility, gentleness, tenderness before God and man, in that meekness of the Lamb of God which is the chief grace of the Christian life. Look at the Corinthians: they had spiritual gifts of prophecy, tongues, etc., yet they were unwilling to be subject one to the other; there was strife as to who should speak first. Don't think that the carnal state is the state of a man in whom there is no good. A man may be a preacher, evangelist, sabbath school teacher, organizer, and yet—alas!—God may say to that man, "Are you not carnal?" Does he not do as much good in the end? No. He may help another to the Christian life but the Christian life he helps him to is such a mixed one that it is

---

[7] 1 Corinthians 1:4-5

feeble and does not stand. The man whose inner life is under the rule of the Spirit, who is himself spiritual, will beget really spiritual children; he will impart the life of God in power. Being able to exercise spiritual gifts is no necessary proof that we are not carnal.

iv. The carnal state brings an incapacity for receiving spiritual truth.

Just note how distinctly Paul says this in writing to the Corinthians. In the first and second chapters he had been speaking about himself, Christ having sent him to preach the cross, not with human wisdom but in the power of the Spirit. Then in the third chapter he speaks about the church and he turns to them and says, "I have received the mystery of God but I cannot tell you." Why not? Were the Corinthians very stupid? No, they were great seekers after wisdom, they prided themselves upon their knowledge. In the passage that I read a short time ago you will remember it said they were "enriched in all knowledge."[8] They were a cultured, thoughtful people. The wisdom of the world was beautiful in their eyes, and yet Paul said, "all your wisdom will not help you."

If I were to speak spiritual truth you would take it into a carnal mind and intellect and it would be an injury to you. There is a terrible mistake made right at this point very often. Paul says, "Before I can write to them, I must settle it in my mind that they are carnal people. I must let them know that they are carnal and bring them to the point of realizing that they are carnal." How often in the church of Christ we preach to people who are carnal, deep spiritual truths; we clothe our thoughts in beautiful words and illustrations; they say, "What a beautiful sermon" and practically it does them very little good. Was not the sermon true? Was not the truth of the Bible in it? Yes, but you preached spiritual truth to carnal people. Friends, as long as the Christian is carnal

---

[8] 1 Corinthians 1:5

don't give him spiritual truth. You must bring him to the point where he recognizes that he is carnal. The carnal state is incapable of receiving spiritual truth.

2. From carnal to spiritual

Paul did not want the Corinthians to rest in the carnal state. No! He wanted them to pass from carnal to spiritual. That is what we need too. And the question comes, how are we to get from the one to the other? Note four of the principal steps:

i. The believer must be convicted and brought to the confession of his being in the carnal state.

You know that before a sinner can be converted, he must be convicted of sin; he must know and confess his transgressions and his lost estate. Just so, believers must see that they are in a wrong state; before they can get into the spiritual life they must be brought under conviction of the shame and evil of this carnal state. There is a great difference between conviction before conversion and this. Then, that which principally occupied the mind was the thought, "I am lost, I am under condemnation;" the great idea was the greatness of his transgressions and the desire to have them pardoned. There were two things that he was not convicted of: that his nature is utterly sinful, the other that there are many hidden heart sins that he has never known.

This is the reason God brings a believer into what might be termed a second conviction. It is most needful that he be fully convicted of two things: the utter impotence of the flesh to do any good; the mighty power of the flesh to work evil. The flesh is ruling him. He has the Spirit of God in him, and why does he yet do these things?

It is just the seventh of Romans, "I am struggling to do right and I cannot."[9] Oh friends, it is when a man is brought under conviction of the utter impotence of the flesh to do good, its helplessness, that he will understand why he lost his temper, and why pride comes up, and why he speaks wrong words. The flesh takes him captive; the law of sin in him binds him hand and foot. Then comes those great hidden sins that the world counts very little, which are seen to be works of the flesh. The Holy Spirit convicts of pride as being of the flesh; unloving thoughts toward wife, or child, or servant; self-pleasing before God and man; and so he needs an entire deliverance, different from that at conversion. Then he was delivered from the curse of sin, now he wants deliverance from the power of sin. Many in the church of Christ will have to cry, "Woe is me, O wretched man that I am, in my flesh dwelleth no good thing."[10] It is simply because the flesh has power that you sin, you must find deliverance. And there is no deliverance but by becoming an entire spiritual man.

ii. The second step is that a man must be made to see and believe that the spiritual life is a possibility.

A great many people will say in a creed that they believe in the Holy Ghost. They have no doubt about the existence of the Holy Ghost and that He is the Third Person of the Blessed God-Head. They are orthodox on all these points; but it is an intellectual belief. They practically do not believe in what the Holy Ghost can do in a believer every day of his life. A man must be brought to see that there is a spiritual life within his reach; that there is a spiritual life which it is his duty to live; that there is a spiritual life he is in need of and may claim. There is a life in the Spirit. Note such expressions as "Walk in the Spirit," "Live in the Spirit," "By the

---

[9] Romans 7:15-20
[10] Romans 7:24,18

Spirit, mortify the deeds of the body."[11] Just take the sixteen verses of the eighth chapter of Romans in which the Holy Spirit is mentioned, and a man must begin to see that God wants him to be a spiritual man. He cannot bear to have me carnal. God commands me to be spiritual and by the grace of God, just as certainly as Christ's blood flowed for my sins, so Christ's Spirit can lead me down into the place of absolute helplessness where He will live in me in His Divine power and renew my whole nature into spiritual.

Oh, take this step before I go further. Reach out at once and begin in a simple act of faith to obey God's call. Say, "O God, a spiritual life is possible, I can become a spiritual man!" Let us begin and believe that the God who gave the Holy Spirit delights in nothing more than to give the Holy Spirit in each of us to live this life.

When a man is convicted of a carnal life and believes in the possibility of a spiritual life, he comes to the third step.

iii. Third, are you willing to give up everything to get the spiritual life?

Then comes the time of struggling. A great many delight to read about the spiritual life, but that is not enough. I must buy. At what price? Give up all. You must sell all to buy the pearl of great price. Come with every sin and every folly, all temper, everything you love, your whole life, and place it in the possession of Christ. Die to everything and be fully given up to God. It is only in the vessel that is fully cleansed that the Holy Spirit can do His work. Here in Chicago the question is often asked, "Will a thing pay?" If it will pay men will undertake anything. If there is one thing that will pay it is to give up everything for God—everything of the flesh—to become a truly spiritual man.

---

[11] Romans 8:1-16

iv. Fourth and last step. When a man says, "I am willing" then he must come in faith and claim it.

It is just faith over again. It is faith from beginning to end. When a man gives up all, he must look up at the Lord Jesus to whom the Father has given the Holy Spirit, claim the promise and believe that he receives it. Bow before God, the Holy One, in deep humility and submission; with faith in His promise, His power, His great love, His near providence—God, who is a spirit and gives the Spirit, will, in the fellowship with Himself, make thee a spiritual man.

May God, in His mercy, open the eyes of all His people to discern the two states of carnal and spiritual. May He bring all who are yet in the carnal state to full conviction and confession. And through them may He bring many to the acceptancy of the full spiritual life He has provided in Christ Jesus.

2. Seven Blessings
(Romans 8:1-16)

We learned this morning from God's Word to the Corinthians that there are two classes of Christians. Paul speaks of some who are carnal and of others who are spiritual. I tried to point out what the life of the carnal Christian is, what a wrong and wretched state it is; and on the other hand, what the steps are by which we can get out of the carnal state into the spiritual. Among these steps I mentioned first of all that a man must be fully convicted of the wrongness of the carnal state, and of the possibilities and blessedness of the spiritual state.

I want, tonight, to speak of the latter and to set before you what God's Word teaches of a life in the Spirit. You know when the Children of Israel got to Kadesh-Barnea they sent out spies to see what the land was like.[12] God expected that when they saw the grapes and heard of the beauty of that land they would all enter in. So, God wants us to look at the spiritual life until we believe that it is indeed to be divided and within our reach.

Later on in these addresses, we shall have occasion to come back to the carnal life and the passage out of it, but I want, by God's help tonight, just to set before you what the life is in the fullness of the Spirit, as God expects His children to live it day by day. I want to take you to a chapter in God's word where it is set before us more plainly than in any other chapter. Romans, the eighth chapter. Let us read the first sixteen verses. You will find in these seven blessings, seven of the blessed fruits of the Spirit in us. I shall point them out as we read.

---

[12] Numbers 13

1. "Who walk not after the flesh but after the Spirit."[13] The whole of our conduct is under the rule of the Spirit.

2. "For the law of the Spirit of life in Christ Jesus hath made me free from the law of sin and death."[14] The Spirit brings us into liberties.

3. "They that are after the Spirit ... ye are in the Spirit ... the Spirit dwells in you."[15] The Christian has a new nature; God's Spirit is in him.

4. "Do mind the things of the Spirit."[16] To be spiritually minded is life and peace. Mind means disposition; to mind the things of the Spirit, to have a spiritual disposition.

5. Vs. 13. "If ye through the Spirit do mortify the deeds of the body ye shall live."[17] The Spirit makes the death to sin an actual reality in our body.

6. "As many as are led by the Spirit of God they are the sons of God."[18] Divine guidance.

7. "Ye have not received the spirit of bondage again to fear, but ye have received the Spirit of adoption."[19] The Spirit beareth witness with our spirit.

What I want to put before you is this: that all we have in this chapter is simply the description of the normal Christian life. This is a thing for every believer. We are sometimes in danger of talking about the baptism of the Spirit, of being filled with the Spirit for

---

[13] Romans 8:1
[14] Romans 8:2
[15] Romans 8:5,9,11
[16] Romans 8:5
[17] Romans 8:13
[18] Romans 8:14
[19] Romans 8:15

service, as though that were all, but it is possible as I pointed out this morning to have baptism of the Holy Spirit for special service and yet be carnal. We want to feel that we must not seek the baptism of the Holy Spirit as a power for work only, but as a far more important matter: we must have the baptism of the Holy Spirit for our whole life. The work must be the outcome of the life.

There are over 100 men in the gold fields of South Africa who have been Christian workers but have now given up their religion for gold. It is possible that at the time of their service they had the Spirit of God, but it was a very superficial work in their hearts and lives. The Holy Spirit had never been allowed to go down into the very depths of their being to establish the life of God through their whole nature. If He had, they would never have gone back. Nothing can take us back when the Holy Spirit gets entire possession of our inner life. I want to show you this evening what provision God has made for you.

You know in England that the nobility when they want their names to be carried down, entail their estate so that it must always go to the eldest son. Often there will be younger sons who get almost nothing. God does not do that. He disinherits none of His sons. He calls all of His children to share alike in the blessed gift of the Holy Spirit. All may not have the same gift of power for work, but all may and must have the fitness for a life full of God. Let us all seek Him.

Let me point you to seven principal thoughts in the passage:

1. *The Christian is a man who walks after the Spirit.*

In Galatians it is said, "If we live in the Spirit let us also walk in the Spirit."[20] "Walk in the Spirit and ye shall not fulfill the lusts of the

---

[20] Galatians 5:25

flesh."[21] My walk is my conduct, what the Bible calls my conversation, my course of life, my external manner of life. Here I am told as a Christian, God will enable me to walk after the Spirit, with the Spirit as my inspiration. Unconverted men walk after the flesh; the flesh leads them and tells them what to do. The Christian can come into the life of the Spirit; in it he acts, in it he walks, he has the continual hidden guidance of the Spirit of God molding and shaping his will and walk.

I may be a minister. If I walk after the Spirit, that does not mean that I am to pray for the Spirit just before I preach, and in other things live after the flesh. No, God calls us to walk in the Spirit at all times. Is not that what you wish? I need the Spirit so that when I sit down at my table, when my temper might be tempted to rise; in my business, in trials of any kind I may feel the power of the Holy Spirit working in me, and moving me. All my walk is to be according to the Spirit. How can I get to that?

2. Paul says in the second verse "For the law of the Spirit of life in Christ Jesus has made me free from the law of sin and death."[22]

In the seventh chapter he speaks of a believer, a regenerated man, who delights in the law of God after the inward man but who finds another law in his members that leads him into captivity to the law of sin and death.[23] I am a prisoner, I am a captive, I want to do good but I cannot. Suppose a husband is in prison and his wife and children are all starving. She writes to him, "Can you not do something to help me?" He writes back, "I long to help you, I would do anything I could to help you, but here I am bound, so that I cannot." This is just like the believer in the seventh chapter of Romans. "I long to obey God but I cannot." Why? Because he is

---

[21] Galatians 5:15
[22] Romans 8:2
[23] Romans 7:22-23

bound with the chains of the flesh, in captivity to the law of sin and
death in his members. But the Spirit sets a man free out of this
captivity. "The law of the Spirit of life hath made me free from the
law of sin and death."

Let us believe there are two powers, the power of the Spirit and the
power of sin. Which is stronger? Many Christians tell me the power
of the flesh is stronger. It is very sad that so many think thus. Paul
tells me, God tells me, that the power of the Holy Spirit is stronger,
and the power of the Holy Spirit can make me free from the law of
sin and death if I trust Him.

It is not here a question of the last root of sin being exterminated.
We believe the tendency to evil remains to the end, but we believe
this word too is literal truth, that the Spirit of life in Christ makes
me free from the law of sin to such extent that it has no power over
me. My enemy is there, but he cannot touch me. After the close of
your Civil War, those who had been slaves could dwell in the
presence of their former masters; the masters were not dead and
yet they could not touch them. Just so the Holy Spirit can take
possession, and in presence of the power of sin the Holy Spirit can
fill the believer and make sin powerless.

Are there not many who serve God under constraint, who have to
force themselves to go and work for God, and then ever feel that
they come far short; they cannot rejoice in the liberty wherewith
Christ has made us free. The Master said, "If the Son make you free
ye shall be free indeed,"[24] but you do not enjoy it. If you believed it,
if you trusted God's word for it, you would begin to long for the
fullness of the Holy Spirit and you would understand that nothing
less than this being made free by the Holy Spirit dwelling in His
fullness in you can enable you to live an inwardly holy life.

---

[24] John 8:36

3. "Ye are not in the flesh but in the Spirit if so be that the Spirit of God dwell in you."[25]

"Of the Spirit," "After the Spirit," "In the Spirit," "The Spirit of God in you." All these expressions are used to express the one thought of the closeness, and the reality of the blessed union by which the Holy Spirit takes possession of me. I am in Him and He is in me just as a man is in the air and the air is in him. The air is in my lungs and I am in the air that surrounds me. The two things go together: I go into the fresh air and the fresh air comes into me. Even so the child of God is taken out of the life of the flesh and taken into the life of the Spirit. The Spirit surrounds him on every side with a divine power that is breathed into him and that constitutes his life. He is in the Spirit and the Spirit is in him. He is after the Spirit and the very nature—the divine nature—of the Spirit is in him.

Have you ever thought about it? How wonderful—the Spirit of God becomes the very spirit of our life! Many people think of the Holy Spirit dwelling in us as a man dwells in a house, the man and the house remain separate existences all the time. There is no organic union, no participation of life or nature between the two. That is not the way with the Holy Spirit. He comes into my very being and just as my thinking and willing and feeling is my very nature, so by the Holy Spirit, I become partaker of the divine nature[26]; He enters deep, deep, into me and pervades my whole inner life. The Spirit of God is in me and I am in the Spirit of God. Ought that not to fill us with a holy fear and a holy joy? Fear lest we should remain ignorant of the truth; joy in the expectation of all we will do. The Spirit who came out from the Father and the Son brings and reveals them to me. And the three persons in the one God-Head through Him come into my heart and so I live in the Spirit.

---

[25] Romans 8:9
[26] 2 Peter 1:4

Oh, believers who do not think it possible to live this blessed life! I will tell you the simple reason: because you do not believe God, do not believe that Almighty God will dwell in you. Will you not begin and say, "if it be true, I may be in the Spirit just as I am in the air, thank God, I think I can lead a holy and blessed life."

4. *"They that are after the Spirit do mind the things of the Spirit"*[27]

What does that word 'mind' mean? Generally, it is used of the intellect, but here it means something else. You know when I speak of a high-minded man, by 'mind' I mean disposition. A large-hearted man is one of a large-hearted disposition. To be a spiritual-minded man is to have the disposition of the Holy Spirit; heavenly-minded is a mind that has the spirit and disposition of heaven. To be spiritually-minded is life and peace. The Holy Spirit is ready to breathe within me the very mind and disposition of Christ; that is what Paul meant in writing to the Philippians, "Let this mind be in you that was in Christ Jesus,"[28] etc.

If the Holy Spirit comes in and takes possession of my disposition, I shall have the mind of Christ. God's word says, "Love thy neighbor as thyself;"[29] you have tried hard but failed because it is not natural. But it is no difficulty to a mother to be gentle and loving because it is her natural disposition to be so. Just so the Holy Spirit will make my disposition spiritual-minded. He lives within me and breathes into me everything that is gentle and Christ-like and humble. He puts it so into me that it becomes my very nature. I can love him whom I hated.

The love of God is indeed a wonderful mystery; when it becomes ours, the more unlovable a man is the more we love him, the more

---

[27] Romans 8:5
[28] Philippians 2:5
[29] Mark 12:31

unworthy a man is the more love is magnified in loving him. You find it so hard to keep your tempers. There is just one reason for this: you are not spiritually minded. The Spirit of God must come and fill you. You may have had Him in some measure, but He must fill you deeper and deeper. He must fill you with the disposition of Jesus so that you become spiritually minded. Christians! Would you not long to have such a disposition that everything about you might be spiritual? The Spirit who dwells in you can and will give if you yield to Him.

5. Vs. 13. "If ye through the Spirit do mortify the deeds of the body ye shall live."[30]

The word "mortify" simply means to cause to die. "If ye make dead the deeds of the body ye shall live." The man who has not given the body over to the Spirit to do His work, what a trouble the body gives him! How much sin comes out of the body! Many Christians never understand that it is the deeds of the body that must be made dead. But it is very hard, and in fact impossible, until we begin to see that it is through the Holy Ghost who is the mighty power of God.

It is a very simple thing eating and drinking a little too much. And is that such a great sin? Ask the Bible. "Whether ye eat or drink do all to the glory of God."[31] Overeating or eating for mere enjoyment, weights and makes the body heavy and unfit for prayer. That is the time the devil can come to you. A man may be living in victory over some sin but through the pleasure of eating, the devil may get power over his flesh. When you think you are only feeding the body, you are feeding the flesh. You are strengthening it by gratifying its appetite. That cannot please God. Temper is very much a sin of the flesh. It is in me. It is my selfhood. A bundle of

---

[30] Romans 8:13
[31] 1 Corinthians 10:31

nerves is nothing but a bundle of self. The Holy Spirit is able to mortify the deeds of the body and to reign through it all with His Divine peace and power. If you want to have the deeds of the body mortified, beware of the lust of the flesh and the lust of the eyes.

Ah, Christians, remember if you want to have your body the temple of the Holy Ghost, if you want to live a holy life, you must be filled with the Spirit. Your body too must be under the power. You might know the mysteries of the heavens, like the apostle Paul, but this could give you no help to live a holy life. God's word has no help for you except as it tells you that you must be filled with the Spirit. You know how Scripture speaks about being baptized into the death of Christ; we must reckon ourselves indeed dead unto sin and alive unto God. It says we are crucified with Christ; we are dead. And then it adds, "mortify therefore your members."[32] My inmost regenerated life is life out of death—a life dead to sin in Christ. And the Spirit of Christ maintains the power of that death in the body.

People say that this is too hard. You know the Christians of old sometimes gave their whole lives to keep down the body; and some of the most earnest would go into solitary caves, and yet there they found themselves tempted more than ever with evil spirits. They were trying to be holy by self-mortification but they did not succeed. "If ye through the Spirit do mortify the deeds of the body ye shall live." If you are willing to claim and receive the power of the Holy Spirit, the thing can be done. It was the Holy Spirit that took Christ to Calvary. It was through the eternal Spirit He offered Himself as a sacrifice unto God.[33] By that eternal Spirit we too, can be led to Calvary, to the place of crucifixion, to the conformity of Christ's death and the experience of its power. Have you ever cried in despair, "Oh, that I might be crucified to the world and dead to sin"? The Holy Spirit will do it! Oh, the blessedness of a life filled with this Spirit!

---

[32] Colossians 3:5
[33] Hebrews 9:14

6. "As many as are led by the Spirit of God they are the sons of God."[34]

There you have the leading of the Holy Spirit. There are a great many people who are always ready to ask, "Do tell me, how can I know the leading of the Holy Spirit? I want to know God's will, I pray, and seek, and cannot get it." They want to know God's will in some perplexing question. I always tell them, you begin at the wrong end. What does a little child do? He comes to his father and says, "I want to be an engineer," the father says, "Yes, my son, but you must learn a number of things before you can be an engineer." The child may say, "I want to be an engineer but I don't want to learn all those things." The father will point out that he must learn to add one, two and three, and so on, before he can be an engineer, and it will take a good long time; he must master the simple things before he can go on to the higher. And so I say to the inquirer, the Holy Spirit wants to lead you in the simpler things of daily life. He wants you in daily life to be spiritually minded. Then you will know the mind of the Spirit in special circumstances. If, in your daily life, you will say, "Lord, let me know what my conduct today should be," then you will be prepared for understanding His leading in times of need. Then He will lead you into deeper things of God's word. Then He will show you how you are to walk.

That is exactly the life of the Lord Jesus. You remember He said, "I cannot do anything of myself, the words I speak are not my own, what the Father showeth me I do,"[35] etc. He was always listening to the voice of God and was led by God. Is it not a wonderful privilege for us? As God says, "As many as are led by the Spirit of God they are the sons of God."

Dear Christians, would you not be willing to sacrifice everything for that—that you might be led by the Spirit? You know God cannot

---

[34] Romans 8:14
[35] John 5:30, John 12:49, John 5:20

abate His requirements. I must give up having any will of my own. I must desire above everything to lead a holy life like Jesus, in dependent, humble waiting upon God. You say that is hard. It is not hard! It is the most blessed life. It is exactly the life Jesus lived. Is it not a privilege to have the blessed God lead and guide me all along, in everything? He has promised to do that.

"As many as are led by the Spirit of God they are the sons of God." Oh, beloved let us realize what this life is! If you speak about the baptism of the Holy Spirit, for service—and I want you to speak about it; I want you to be filled with the Holy Spirit for your work— remember there is something of far deeper importance. It is that your whole life, from moment to moment, bear the mark of being led by the Spirit, of being spiritually-minded. The Spirit of Jesus makes you like Jesus. By the Holy Ghost you can live a Christlike life.

7. *"Ye have not received the spirit of bondage again to fear, but ye have received the spirit of adoption whereby we cry Abba, Father. The Spirit dwelleth with our spirit."*[36]

What Spirit? The Spirit that has been described in the previous verses as leading us, making us spiritually minded, mortifying the deeds of the body: that is the spirit of adoption. This is the Spirit that will bear witness that I am a son of God. Many people talk about the witness of the Holy Spirit they received when they believed. I do not say they are not children of God, but they do not live like it. If we want the spirit of adoption by which every day we can have that assurance and evidence that can confidently say, "Abba, Father," then we must be in the Spirit and must walk after the Spirit. If by Him I am living, if He dwell in and possess me, if I be of the Spirit and after the Spirit, if the Spirit is mine, my life will be one of increasing joy and fellowship with God.

---

[36] Romans 8:15-16

How gently He leads me, how close He keeps by me! Through Him God fulfills the word that He spoke to the elder son in the parable of the prodigal son: "Son, thou art ever with me, and all I have is thine."[37] That becomes a possession, an experience, made real by the Holy Ghost, that makes the spiritual, heavenly minded man. "Abba, Father," I do not have to try and feel, or claim, or struggle for the relationship, but the Everlasting God reveals Himself to me as a Father. So the Living Father makes us to know what it means to be dwelling in love and dwelling in God, and what all the promises about the Holy Spirit mean.

"The Father shall send the Comforter that He may abide with you forever."[38] Beloved Christians, there is a wonderful life which the Holy Spirit makes intensely true. It is a real Canaan life.[39] It is indeed a solemn, precious thought. God's Holy Spirit can make all God's promises and provisions in Christ our experience.

Who are ready to come into this life tonight and claim the heritage as the child of God? Who will cry: "I am going to ask that Romans 8:1-16 shall be literally fulfilled in my life!"

Let me suggest four simple steps. Say tonight:

1. I *must* be filled with the Spirit. God commands it. My soul needs it. The Spirit longs for it. Christ will do it. The world needs it. I cannot live aright without it. I must be filled with the Spirit!

2. I *may* be filled with the Spirit. God does not give a "must" without a "may." God does not say you must live holy, without saying you may, you can live holy. Say, "I may." God has promised it. Christ has purchased it. The Word reveals it. Thousands have experienced it. I may be filled with the Spirit!

---

[37] Luke 15:31
[38] John 14:16
[39] The life of the Promised Land

3. I *would* be filled with the Spirit. Say: Lord, my heart longs for it. Begin to say: I give up everything, oh God—self, sin, self-will, self-confidence, the flesh; I give up everything. I would be filled with the Holy Spirit. Lord God, set Thy mark upon me; I am an empty vessel waiting to be filled. I would be filled with the Holy Spirit. I am ready.

4. I *shall* be filled with the Holy Spirit. God has promised it to me. I have a right to say I shall be filled with the Spirit. Say that tremblingly and very, very humble. I confess I am carnal, I have felt my sinfulness, I confess my sin. My heart is willing for it; I am going to trust God for it. Oh God, Thou doest above what I can ask or think[40], I give myself to Thee entirely, I trust Thee forever, I give myself up fully and I claim the filling of the Holy Spirit. Thou givest it.

---

[40] Ephesians 3:20

3. The Fruit of the Spirit is Love
(Galatians 5:22)

Last night I tried to put before you what a life filled with the Holy Spirit may be, but more from the doctrinal side. These expressions were found in Romans, 8th chapter, "Walk in the Spirit," "Being made free by the Spirit from the law of sin and death," "Being in the Spirit," "Having the Spirit dwelling in us," "Through the Spirit mortifying the deeds of the body," "Being led by the Spirit," "Having the Spirit of adoption." All these are truths which have to be appropriated and assimilated and worked out in actual life. I want this morning to look at the matter more from the practical side, and to show you how this life will show itself in our daily walk and conduct.

Under the Old Testament you know the Holy Spirit often came upon men as a Divine Spirit of revelation, to reveal the mysteries of God, or for power to do the work of God. But he did not then dwell in them. Now, as I said yesterday morning, many just want the Old Testament gift of power for work but know very little of the New Testament gift of the indwelling Spirit, animating and renewing the whole life.

We saw last night that when God gives the Holy Spirit, His great object is the formation of holy character. We saw that it was a gift of a holy mind and spiritual disposition, and that we need above everything else to say, "I must have the Holy Spirit sanctifying my whole inner life if I am really to live for God's glory." You might say that when Christ promised the Spirit to the disciples, He did so that they might have power to be witnesses. True, but then they received the Holy Ghost in such heavenly power and reality that He took possession of their whole being at once, and so fitted them as holy men for doing the work with power as they had to do it. Christ spoke of power to the disciples, but it was the Spirit filling their whole being that worked the power.

I wish to speak this morning upon the passage found in Galatians 5:22: "The fruit of the Spirit is love." We read that "Love is the fulfilling of the whole law,"[41] and my desire is to speak to you this morning on love as a fruit of the Spirit with a twofold object.

1. Let us try ourselves by this word

One is that this word may be a searchlight in our hearts and give us a test by which to try all our thoughts about the Holy Spirit and all our experience of the holy life. Let us try ourselves by this word. Has this been your daily habit, to seek the being filled with the Holy Spirit as the Spirit of love? "The fruit of the Spirit is love." Has it been your experience that the more you have of the Holy Spirit the more loving you become? In claiming the Holy Spirit you should make this the first object of your expectation, the Holy Spirit comes as a Spirit of love. Oh, if this were true in the church of Christ how different her state would be! May God help us this morning to just get hold of this simple heavenly truth: that the fruit of the Spirit is a love which appears in the life, and that just as the Holy Spirit gets real possession of the life, the heart will be filled with real, Divine, universal love.

To understand this fully let us remember that God from whom the Spirit comes is love. Love is not a mere attribute of God, but God *is* love, and because this Holy Spirit comes as the Spirit of God, He comes as the Spirit of love. What does it mean that God is love? You have in the 13th chapter of 1 Corinthians the most perfect definition of love. "Love seeketh not its own."[42] It goes out of itself and lives in its object, etc. Love longs to commend itself to and

---

[41] Romans 13:10
[42] 1 Corinthians 13:5

bless the object of its love. Therefore, it was an absolute necessity in the idea of a perfect God that He should have a Son to whom He could communicate Himself. We cannot conceive of God—who is love—alone, He must have a Son to whom He can communicate Himself and with whom we can have fellowship. So, God is love. And in the everlasting intercourse of the Trinity, the Spirit is the bond of fellowship between the Father and Son. The Holy Spirit is the overflowing and interchange of the love between Father and Son. He is the very life of Deity; if that Spirit comes to us, He comes in no other way than as the Spirit of love.

God is love, not only *to* Christ, but *in* Christ God created the world that He might pour out His love upon it and that He might give to all His creatures just as much of His love as they each are capable of receiving. God is love. God created angels and men that they might enjoy fellowship with Him, His love permeating and filling their whole being. When man had fallen, when sin had darkened this love of God in man, what did He do? He gave His own Son to the death to restore it. To that fallen world God gave His Son in a new way, in the flesh to prove to man the power of His love. And with His Son, He gave His life, His joy, His glory, His holiness, His power, His blessedness; in Christ He gives it all. God is love, ever delighting to give and communicate Himself. Love is the essential nature of God; with the Holy Spirit coming from this God, must we not expect that He will fill us with love?

Sin has robbed us of love. You know that God created man, male and female, that they might live a life of love even as God lives in love, and they might be happy in love. When sin came it destroyed the love. You know how easily Adam put the blame upon his wife[43], how speedily Cain killed Abel[44], how soon the world became filled with wickedness; how true it is that since that time the world is full of divisions, and strife, of sin and unrighteousness. Love vanished

---

[43] Genesis 3:12
[44] Genesis 4:12

from the world. There may have been beautiful examples of love even among the heathen but only as a little remnant of what has been lost. The worst thing sin ever did was: it made men selfish and selfishness cannot love. Selfishness can do something that is called love; it can lead me to love someone who pleases me or makes me happier, but that is not real love. The true unselfish love that loves the unworthy or unlovable, sin destroyed. To bring this love back to us, Jesus came.

He came as the manifestation of Divine love. We read before He went to be crucified that, "Having loved His own that were in the world, He loved them unto the end."45 Christ's life with His disciples was one of love. His influence was personal. His whole intercourse with them was one of love. In the 13th chapter of John you will remember Christ said unto them, "A new commandment I give unto you, that ye love one another."46 This commandment differed from all other commandments, and yet it contained them all. It was a new commandment Christ alone could give, because He had revealed a new love, and would give it in the heart by giving His Spirit there. "I tell you, love one another." "By this shall men know that ye are my disciples if you love one another."47 In the 15th chapter He says again, "This commandment have I given unto you that ye love one another."48

In the 17th chapter He prayed, "That they may be one as we are one, that the world may know Thou hast loved me and hast sent me and hast loved them as Thou hast loved me."49 The world is to know the love of God through Christ by our love to one another. So, we are taught that the great mark of the believer is that he is to be a man of love. Dear friends, how little the world understands that; how little the church understands that; how little it is preached or

45 John 13:1
46 John 13:34
47 John 13:35
48 John 15:12

proved in practice that love is actually the chief thing for every
believer to set his heart upon. How little can believers say before
God, "Thou knowest I pray for one thing, fill me with love; I study
one thing, how can I be filled with love?" The Lord Jesus came to
bring love back to the world. He did so when He died on Calvary, it
was the triumph and the revelation of love. And now He calls us to
dwell and to walk in love. He demands that though a man hate you
still you love him. True love cannot be conquered by anything in
heaven or upon the earth. The more hatred there is the more love
triumphs through it all and shows its true nature. This is the love
that Christ commanded His disciples to exercise.

John in his epistle says that Christ laid down His life for us,
therefore we ought to lay down our life for the brethren.[50] How
little men understand that! Look at the disciples. How often there
were dissensions among them; more than once they disputed as to
who should be chief in the kingdom. There was pride because of
their want of love. Love is humility. Love says, I only exist to be a
blessing to others. Love cannot be selfish; it loves as Jesus loved.
The disciples whom Christ had chosen had to be taught many
things, but one chief object was to let us see what human nature is
and how incapable it is of the higher life, of love like Christ's, until
the Holy Spirit comes.

2. Let us be filled with the Holy Spirit

When Jesus Christ had revealed love on earth and had done the
work of redeeming love, the Holy Spirit came from heaven to bring
His love down to our hearts. We ought to think of Pentecost, as it
brought the very life and love of Jesus into the hearts of His
disciples. So it was that Peter could speak out of the very Spirit of
Jesus.

---

[49] John 17:22-23
[50] 1 John 3:16

The disciples learned not only to love each other, but even their enemies. We talk of their boldness because that comes out in contrast to their cowardice; it was the redeeming love of Christ that came to take possession of them, which the Holy Spirit brought down from heaven. In the second and the fourth chapters of Acts we read that "they were of one heart and one soul."[51] During the three years they had walked with Christ they never had one heart and one soul. All Christ's teaching could not make them of one heart and one soul. But the Holy Spirit comes from heaven and sheds the love of God in their hearts[52] and they are of one heart and one soul. The same Holy Spirit that brought the love of heaven into their hearts must fill us too. Nothing less will do. Even as Christ did, one might preach love for three years with the tongue of an angel, that would not teach any man to love unless the power of the Holy Spirit come upon him to bring the love of heaven into his heart. If we wait upon the Holy Spirit and yield ourselves to Him, He will fill us with the love of God.

Look at this as we have it here in our text. It is in our daily life and conduct that the fruit of the Spirit is love; from that there comes all the graces and virtues in which love is manifested: joy, peace, long, suffering, gentleness, goodness; no sharpness or hardness in your tone, no unkindness or selfishness; meekness before God and man. You see that all these are the gentler virtues. I have often thought as I read those words in Colossians, "Put on therefore as the elect of God, holy and beloved, bowels of mercies, kindness, humbleness of mind, meekness, longsuffering,"[53] that if we had written, we should have put in the foreground the manly virtues—zeal, courage and diligence; but we need to see how the gentler, the most womanly virtues are specially connected with dependence upon the Holy Spirit. These are indeed heavenly graces. They never were found in the heathen world. Christ was needed to come from

---

[51] Acts 2:42-47, Acts 4:32-35
[52] Romans 5:5
[53] Colossians 3:12

heaven to teach us. Your blessedness is longsuffering, meekness, kindness; your glory is humility before God. The fruit of the Spirit, that He brought from heaven out of the heart of the crucified Christ and that He gives in our heart, is first and foremost love.

Don't you see that if this is really true, our great desire in asking to be filled with the Holy Spirit, our great study now that we are talking about the filling of the Spirit and how to be filled with power by the Spirit, our great aim and study must be to get hold of this thought: if we are to have the Holy Spirit we must give up ourselves, give up self to live the life of love.

How sadly has this been wanting? What shall I say about the divisions throughout the Church of Christ? How the most precious truths given by Christ to unite us have been made barriers of separation. Take the Lord's Supper. What terrible quarrels between Reformed Lutherans about the meaning of the simple words, "This is my body."[54] What was meant as a bond of union is a badge of separation. Alas! how little the Divine beauty, the Divine supremacy of love has been seen. Our doctrines, our creeds have been more important than love. In these later times, even the baptism of the Holy Spirit is a cause of separation. Let us learn not to expect that everyone should think the same or express themselves in the same way; let our first care be to exercise love, gentleness, kindness. We often think we are valiant for the truth, and we forget that God's word commands us to speak the truth in love.

How often one hears that even away out among the heathen or mission stations there are too often divisions and coldness among those who are working for God. Because of differences of temperament or opinion, estrangements and jealousies come in and love waxes cold. What a sad thing in the church that earnest Christians who have given up all for Christ have never learned the

---

[54] Luke 22:19

mystery of love.

Is it any different at home? Is there not often, in the circles where we meet together, in church councils, and committees, in missions and associations, a want of that love among fellow-workers, which is the true mark of the presence of the Holy Ghost? Is there not often harsh judgment, evil-speaking, etc., all because the love of Christ has not been allowed to take complete possession. Is there not often even in the family the outburst of temper and haste? Alas! We have not learned to love, have not even learned to count love the chief fruit of the Spirit. We must learn to take this word as the true test of life in the Spirit. All our desire to be filled with the Spirit must center here: to have self sunk down in willingness and humility, and to have the love of God and Jesus become the life of our life.

I want to lead you to the life in which love is supreme, in which love shall bow you down in such deep humility that go where you will and let man do what they will, you shall say, "By the help of God I must love." Let us bring our whole life to the looking glass of this word of God. Let us think of the church and Christians around us. When you have looked around well then look at yourself and say, "Oh God, I ask Thee so often to fill Thy church with the Holy Spirit. Have I been filled with the Spirit of love?" You know what John says, "No man hath seen the Father at any time. If we love one another God dwells in us."[55] That is, I cannot see God, but as a compensation I can see my brother and if I love him, God dwells in me.

Is that really true? That I cannot see God, but I must love my brother, and God will dwell in me. Loving my brother is the way to real fellowship with God. You know what John further says in that most solemn test, 1 John, 4:20, "If a man says he loves God and hates his brother he is a liar; for he that loveth not his brother

---

[55] 1 John 4:12

whom he hath seen, how can he love God whom he hath not seen?" There is a brother, a most unlovable man. He worries you every time you meet him. He is of the very opposite disposition to yours. You are a careful business man and you have got to do with him in your business. He is most untidy, unbusinesslike. You say, "I cannot love him." Oh friends, you have not learned the lesson that Christ wanted to teach above everything. Let a man be what he will you are to love him. Love is to be the fruit of the Spirit all the day and every day.

Yes, listen, if a man loves not his brother whom he hath seen, if you don't love that unlovable man whom you have seen, how can you love God whom you have not seen? You can deceive yourself with beautiful thoughts about loving God. You must prove your love to God by your love to your brother; that is the one standard God will judge your love to Him by. If the love of God is in your heart you will love your brother. The fruit of the Spirit is love. The first thing you need, if you want to be filled with the Spirit, in any real, full sense of the word: you must not only have Him take possession of your will, but you must yield up your heart and life to be filled with the Spirit of love.

Nothing can enable you to live such a life of love but the fullness of the Holy Spirit. The two texts are inseparably connected. "Be filled with the Spirit,"[56] "The fruit of the Spirit is love."[57] If a man wants to have the fruit of an apple tree, he must plant the apple tree. You must have the tree if you want the fruit. If you want to be filled with the love of God, you must be filled with the Spirit. You must come with the humble confession of how little you have loved, or even desired to be full of love. You have sought for the power of the Holy Spirit in your work in pride and selfishness You have not given up yourself to Him to be filled first of all with love, with gentleness and humility and meekness. Oh, come and make

---

[56] Ephesians 5:18
[57] Galatians 5:2

confession, and let Christ cleanse you from the selfishness and pride and unlovingness! Seek to be filled with the Spirit for a daily life of humility and love, and the power of the Spirit for service will come.

Brother, do you want to be filled with the Spirit of God? Is it true? Do you really want to be filled with love that you may be the humblest, gentlest of men, so that everyone may know that you are a disciple by the love you have? Brethren, if we love one another God dwelleth in us[58] and we in God, and then we can be perfected in love. Is that an attainment of ours? It is a gift, a bestowment of the Holy Spirit.

I hope, in the evening, to speak about the hindrances to this life, how it comes that this life in the Spirit, this love of the Spirit, walking after the Spirit, made free by the Spirit, indwelt by the Spirit, having the witness of the Spirit—what it is that hinders these in our life. How it is that Christ has given the Spirit, that the Spirit is in the church, and her life is so feeble?

But meantime, let us first in confession ask God to forgive us our shortcomings; let us in prayer and faith yield ourselves and let God fill us with the Spirit of love. Let us even now absolutely and entirely give ourselves to be just vessels filled with the love of God. Let us even now say to God that we accept the lesson, that the Spirit comes to fill us with the love of heaven, with a love that makes loving others the one joy of our life; that we yield ourselves to it, and that by His grace we will make this our one object and desire. May God write it in our hearts. The Holy Spirit's fruit and chief work is to give Christ and the love of God in us for our everyday life. By His grace we can live lives of unceasing love.

---

[58] 1 John 4:12

4. The Self-life: the hindrance to the Spiritual Life
(Matthew 16:24)

Let me begin, for the sake of any who are here for the first time, by saying a word about what we are doing and where we are.

These meetings are not simply for the discussion or exposition of scriptural truth, but have all a very definite, practical object. Their starting point is very simple. Many Christians feel that their life is not right. They long to have their life put right, and ask the question, "Is it possible to live as God would have us do?" We desire to come and show them exactly what it is that is wrong, and exactly what it is that God is willing and able to do for them, and then to bring them to take the step by which they pass out of the wrong state into the life that is well pleasing to God. This is our work, and I do pray you in great love, everyone, to set aside any tendency to come and merely to listen to the exposition of truth. We have such a terrible habit of going to church to listen and to learn and to think, while the heart often remains untouched, that we get into the habit of listening to the most solemn things without any practical result. Let us try and come into God's presence tonight, and in His presence to say, "If there is anything wrong about me, I pray God to set it right." Let there be in our hearts a hungering after righteousness.

We began yesterday morning by looking at the two sides of the Christian life: the carnal, fleshly side in which a believer is continually sinning, and then at the spiritual side in which the Holy Spirit helps a man to conquer and makes a man really a spiritual man. Yesterday evening we went on to look at the spiritual side and we found in Romans 8 the description of what the Holy Spirit will

do for a believer who gives way to Him. The Holy Spirit will make
him a free man, free from the law of sin and death. The Holy Spirit
will dwell in him, will lead him and teach him to walk after Him as
his guide. The Holy Spirit will come into him as a Divine life power
to mortify and make dead the deeds of the body, and the Holy
Spirit will come into him to bear a definite, heavenly, living witness
that He is in him. This morning we went further. How will such a
life look when a man has to act it out in his daily walk, and we took
one word as the standard God gives: "The fruit of the Spirit is
love."[59] We said if the Holy Spirit comes and fills a man, the man
will live a life full of love amid all difficulties and trials and
temptations.

And now this evening comes the question: "If that be true, if the
Holy Spirit will set me free from the law of sin and death; if the
Holy Spirit will mortify the deeds of the body, why is it that I do
not live that life? If love be the fruit of the Holy Spirit and I have
the Holy Spirit given me in conversion, why is it I do not live such a
life of perfect love, and that so few live it? There must be some
terrible hindrance." And so there is. The hindrance is just one
word, one little word of four letters: S-E-L-F. The life of God and
the life of Christ and the life of the Holy Spirit are all waiting to
come into you. But on one condition: you must lose your own life.
Give it up and God will give you the new life. But if you allow self to
live in you and have its way even partially, it hinders the work of
the Holy Spirit and though you have the Holy Spirit in you as a
child of God He cannot do His work in power.

Now I want to tell you how you can get rid of this hindrance. My
text is Matthew 16:24. "Then said Jesus unto His disciples, if any
man will come after me, let him deny himself and take up his cross
and follow me." What must he do? He must deny himself; he must
deny self. "If a man wants to be my disciple, he must deny himself
and he must take up his cross and follow me." We all, by nature,

---

[59] Galatians 5:2

follow self. Every man does it. It is natural. Christ says we must give up self, must forever give up listening to self, and listen to Him alone. Take Him in the place of self, give up the life of self and take Him to be your life.

Let us try and understand the connection in which this wonderful word comes to us. You remember how in Caesarea Philippi, Christ asked His disciples, "Whom do men say that I, the Son of Man, am?"[60] They gave Him the different answers that men were giving, and He then said, "But whom say ye that I am?" Peter answered for the rest, "Thou art the Christ, the Son of the living God." And listen to what Christ said, "Blessed art thou, Simon Barjona, because thou knowest this. Thou art blessed because thou knowest that I am the Son of God." And what more does He say? "Flesh and blood has not revealed this unto you but my Father which is in heaven." God, my Father, has been teaching you by His Holy Spirit and you have learned that I am the Son of God. The disciples did not learn it in their catechism in those days; their mothers did not teach it to them; Christ Himself did not say in so many words, "Now remember, I am the Son of God." But He lived as the Son of God, and God taught them to know Him as Christ.

Then Christ goes on and says those two wonderful things. "Upon this rock will I build my church,"[61] and "I will give unto thee the keys of the kingdom of heaven." Think of those four things spoken to Peter. "Blessed art thou, Simon Barjona," "The Father Himself hath revealed it to thee," "On this rock I will build My church," and "I will give unto thee the keys of the kingdom of heaven." And now what comes? Peter is up in the heights. Peter has learned a great heavenly lesson. And what comes now? Christ begins to tell them, "You must know what must come. They are going to take me and kill me. I will have to be crucified but the third day I will rise

[60] Matthew 16:13-17
[61] Matthew 16:17-18

again."[62] Peter said, "God forbid. Far be that from Thee." In the margin it is properly translated "Pity thyself." Peter says, "Have mercy upon thyself. Why dost thou speak thus, Lord? Pity thyself. That shall never be." But Christ says, "Get thee behind me, Satan."[63] It is such a hellish thing that you have said, it is Satan that has taught you.

Will you learn a lesson now? The same man who an hour ago had been saying things that God had taught him began to say things that the Devil had taught him. What a wonderful thing is a converted but unsatisfied man; he has the Spirit of God in him but he has a deal of the Devil in him, too. Then Christ says, after having spoken about His own cross and His own death, "If any man will come after me, let him take up his cross."[64] That means "Peter, it is not only I that have got to die, but you too. Not only I must be crucified, but you must take up your cross. Peter, you are frightened at the thought that I am going to be crucified, but you have to be crucified too." Poor Peter. "If a man wants to be my disciple, he must deny himself and must take up his cross and he must follow me." What a come down for Peter. Peter was up in the heavens. Peter was living in the higher life, rejoicing in that wonderful word—that Christ calls him a blessed man because he knew that He was the Son of God. And why this come down? Just because Peter has not given up all his thoughts to the teaching of God and the Holy Spirit. Peter knows a great deal about Christ and his kingdom of glory, but he does not believe in His crucifixion. There are so many Christians who believe in a thousand wonderful and beautiful things about Christ but they do not believe the chief thing of all: that of taking their cross and being crucified with Jesus. Listen, this word of Jesus teaches us, as well as Peter, what it is that hinders us from understanding Him and enjoying Him, and He teaches us how to get rid of this trouble.

---

[62] Matthew 16:21-22
[63] Matthew 16:23
[64] Matthew 16:24

I want to speak to you this evening about self. Let me ask these questions:

1. Where does it come from, this self that has got to be denied and crucified?
2. What are its works?
3. How can it be conquered?
4. What have I got to do?

1. Where does this self come from?

In the first place what is this self? Christ says, "Deny self." What does that mean? Peter, instead of denying self, denied Jesus. When Christ was being led before Caiaphas, three times he said, "I do not know the man. I have nothing to do with Him."[65] And he said that with an oath. If any man were to say to you, "You have stolen my watch," you would be indignant and would deny the charge. Even so Peter denied Jesus. Jesus had told him to do just the opposite. "Peter, there is one thing you must deny and that is your own self, your own life, your own will."

But where did I get that self from? Did not God create that self in me? Of course He did! Every man and angel has got a self that comes from God's hands. God gave me a self-determining power by which I can say what I want to do with myself, and what for? That every day I may come to God and bring myself for him to fill, and find my blessedness in waiting upon Him and receiving of His fullness. But what a ruin sin has wrought!

Listen for a moment while I speak to you of something that was, before ever man came on this world. The throne of God was surrounded by bright spirits, all pure and perfect. One of the

---

[65] Matthew 26:72

brightest of these pure spirits began to look at himself and wonder
at all the beauty and glory God had given him.[66] He admired
himself and pride came into his heart and he began to say, "I am as
God." He turned his desire from God to self; he thought, "It is not
right that I should be subject to this God." And he lifted up himself
and said, "I, the morning star, the prince of light, am I not the chief
among the powers of heaven?" He turned away from God to self
and pride entered his heart, and he fell out of light into darkness,
and was changed from an angel into a devil, from the brightness of
heaven into the blackness and outer darkness of everlasting hell.

That is what pride—that is what self—did for that angel. Instead of
turning to God he turned to himself and he fell. Then God, to
restore all this glory, created man that in man His own Son might
show forth His glory. He said to man, "I have given you a self, but
let that self always turn to me and you shall always stand in the
light. Do my will and I will fill you with life and blessing
everlasting." But alas, the Devil came to man because he hated him
as he thought of what man might become as the king of the world.
He came to Eve and said, "If you eat of that fruit you will be like
God."[67] He not only spoke these words, but in and with these words
he breathed into her ear and heart the very poison of hell, his own
hellish pride. He said to her, "You can be like God, go and eat of
that tree." Alas, she and Adam harkened, and the very poison of
hell entered into their blood, and that self that lifted itself against
God and turned away from Him became their nature.

And so you and I, who are born of that Adam and Eve, we have in
us a self that exalts itself against God. We know too little what an
evil nature we have within. We have an evil nature that exalts itself
against God and over our fellow men. The whole history of the
human race is nothing but one great struggle, man against man,
each trying to exalt himself higher than the other. One wants more

[66] Isaiah 14:12-15
[67] Genesis 3:5

power, another more learning, another more culture, another more pleasure than anyone else around. Alas! Self is the God that rules the world. There is not one exception.

Oh, if we were but conscious that we have this evil self within us how we would cry, "Deliver me from this monster, O, my God." If there were to come creeping along here a poisonous snake and making straight for someone, how we would jump away and say, "Kill that beast, deliver me from its poison." But alas, we are blind and run into our danger.

A little child has sometimes been known to play with a snake. I know a home in South Africa, where the mother was away at church and had left a colored girl in charge of her little baby just learning to creep and a sister a few years old. The baby was playing on the floor. A beautifully colored but poisonous snake came into the room and lifting its head made ready to strike. The little child, all unconscious of its danger, crept along toward what looked so beautiful. As the snake was looking at it, just ready to strike, the colored girl rushed from behind and seized the child. The child wished to play with that beautifully colored snake. It knew not of the poison.

We have within us a self that has its poison from Satan, that has its poison from hell and yet we cherish and nourish it. What do we not do to please self and nourish self, and we make the devil within us strong. This is the reason why Christ calls us entirely to deny self. To deny self means that you must have nothing to do with him. If you did not steal that watch you must deny it, you reject with indignation the charge, the statement, that you stole it. So, you must reject self. You ask why. Christ says you must take a cross and nail self to the cross. You ask why. Ah, you will never do what Christ says until you see the satanic origin of self, as a horrible rebellion against God. That is its origin, it comes out of hell and drags us back to hell.

2. What are the works of self?

Now look at its works. Look in your own life. What are the works of self? They are chiefly these three: self-will, self-trust and self-exaltation.

i. First let us look at self-will. God created me with a will, and there is nothing in man more noble than a will. Sometimes people speak about having a broken will or too strong a will. If my will was ten times as strong as it is, it would not be too strong if it is given up to God. It is the great power with which a man can serve God. If it is not given up to God, then the Devil has power to move it and self leads that will continually to sin against God. Self-will rules in the life of every natural man. He says, "I do what I like and I have a right to do what I like." But I find among Christians that there are hundreds, who, if you ask, "Did ever you understand that when you became a Christian it was on the condition that you promise never to seek your own will?" They will all tell you they never understood that. But that is just what Christ demands.

You are to do nothing but what God wills. You are to give up your will; self is to have no say in your life. That is the whole secret of salvation, to give up your will, your self, to God. His will is the manifestation of what is in His heart, and if I take my will like an empty cup and say, "Fill my will with Thy will," then I live a blessed life. Many say, "I think I am a Christian and I must of course do the will of God in important things, but in the little things I cannot help following my own will." No. Self is the cause of all our sin against God, and all our wretchedness. Self-pleasing is another of the works of self. The whole life of man and nature has the pleasing of self as its moving principle. And even Christians seek far more to please themselves than to please God. No wonder that self becomes strong and that for its sake we sin unceasingly against the law of love to God and man.

ii. Another work of self is self-confidence. I do not know a more remarkable example than Peter. Christ said to Peter, "Before the cock shall crow, thou shalt deny me thrice."[68] Peter said, "They may all forsake Thee but I will never leave Thee," and yet he denied Christ with an oath. How did that come? Simply from self-confidence. Peter could not believe of himself that he would deny his Lord. He said, "Thou knowest Lord that I love Thee. I have stood so much persecution for Thy sake. I will never deny Thee. I will go to the death with Thee." What was that but self-confidence? He trusted in himself and he fell.

A young person often says, "Six months ago I gave myself to the Lord and I had such a bright and happy time serving Jesus, but some way or other I got cold and went back and what is the reason?" My answer always is, "Only one thing: you trusted yourself." He says, "No, I certainly did not. I felt that I was a poor feeble creature and could do nothing. I did not trust myself." Ah, but my friend you did. If you had trusted Christ, He never could have let you fall. You trusted in yourself. You trusted in your earnestness, in your integrity or something in yourself, and then came all the trouble. Just so with many of you who tell me, "I cannot live the life I want to live." Here is the simple reason: you have been trusting self, trusting to be able by mere effort and mere watchfulness to gain the victory. If you trusted Christ, you would not fall. You have not given up self to the death, to trust in God alone. Does not your heart begin to say, "God have mercy upon me and deliver me from self. If it has been self that has been tempting me to look away from Jesus, that has been coming between Jesus and myself, oh God deliver me."

iii. The third form of self is self-exaltation, pride. Jesus said, "How can ye believe, who take honor one from another." I am not speaking now of the people of the world. All the wretched history of the world is owing to pride. But I am speaking about Christians. How much of touchiness there is about our position. If a man does

---

[68] Matthew 26:33-34

not give me the honor I think I ought to have; if he puts me down to a lower place than I expect, how sensitive I am. How much envy and jealousy there is. Where does this come from? Self-exaltation.

I ask you believers, do not you know what it is to have a heart in which there is constantly coming in the thought, "There I was clever. I knew how to manage those folks. There I made a beautiful prayer." How often those things are entertained and allowed free passage for a time. How often in the presence of God we exalt ourselves. A man can be proud about a very small matter. He can be proud of a fine head of hair, a fine suit of clothes, his learning or money. There is nothing on earth that a man cannot be proud about. A man may ride on a very fine horse and be proud about that. The beast does not make the man a bit better and yet he is proud about it. That is just the way the Devil befools a man. This accursed self from hell is at the root of all this. A seeking of our own honor. God's word says, "God resisteth the proud."[69] Self as seen has corrupted it, and is in its very nature proud and can be nothing else; therefore Christ says, deny self. Does not your heart begin to cry, "How can I get free from self and sin?"

3. How can it be conquered?

How can it be conquered? Christ tells us: "Let a man deny himself and take up his cross and follow me."[70] He puts the three words together, but they all amount to the same thing.

The first is, "Let him deny himself." Let him say, "I have nothing to do with self. I will not listen to it. I will ignore it." That is what Peter said when he denied Christ: "I do not want to be connected with Christ or have anything to do with Him." So, we must say to self, "I have nothing to do with it."

---

[69] James 4:6
[70] Matthew 16:24

Then Christ says, "Take up the cross." The cross always means death. Christ could not explain that to them further. They would not have understood Him. But Christ meant, "Just as I have got to give up my life and be crucified, you will have to be crucified spiritually." And that is what Paul says, "I am crucified with Christ. No longer I but Christ liveth in me."[71]

And, "Follow me." Oh, that blessed word! It must be instead of myself, Jesus, Himself. "Follow me." Here is a choice you have to make between these two. Shall I follow self or follow Jesus? Please self or please Jesus? Deny self or deny Jesus? Remember that solemn lesson of Peter. He would not deny self and what did he come to? He denied Jesus. If you do not deny self utterly you will be denying Jesus every day. You will tell the world, "I have nothing to do with Jesus just now, I am pleasing myself."

Now Christian, come tonight and make the wonderful exchange. Come and begin to understand what a blessed thing it would be instead of self to follow Jesus. Peter did follow Jesus, though with many failures, and where did Christ take him? He took him to that place where he denied his Lord that he might learn to know himself thoroughly. He took him to Gethsemane to show him how little he could watch for one hour; then to the cross to show him how little he could suffer with him. Then He took him to the resurrection and showed Himself as the living Christ, who breathed His Spirit into him; then He took him to the ascension mount and said, "I am going to heaven and the Spirit and the fire will come." He led him to the place where he received the fullness of the Holy Spirit and then and not until then was self dethroned.

How is the reign of self to be cast out? How am I to be delivered from this secret power that I cannot see or root out? Christ says, "Deny self, take up your cross and follow me." Deny self. Take up the cross and say, "I desire to be crucified with Christ; I desire to be

---

made conformable to His death," then follow Christ with your whole heart. Christ will come in and rule.

You know the story of the strong man who kept his house until a stronger came and cast him out.[72] But the stronger one did not stay to dwell. The house was cleansed and garnished but empty. After a time, the evil spirit with seven others came in and dwelt there. It is not enough to cast out self; it will not help you unless He comes in; Christ the stronger must come in and dwell there, and then He keeps the house in safety. Let us all deny that cursed self; take up the cross and follow Him. He will take us to the place of safety and victory.

4. What have I got to do?

And now comes a few words as to what we must do. Can a man in one moment deny self and be freed from it, or is it the work of a lifetime? Both. You can tonight, if God gives you a sight of the accursedness of self and what self has really been doing all the years of your Christian life, in one step take your place in the position of a man who utterly denies self and give yourself to be possessed by Jesus. You can do that in one minute. Many do not do this because they are not ready. They are not willing to confess they have no true insight; that self is the only cause of their sin. But I ask you what else can be the cause of all these sins that have made you unhappy? Temper, pride, willfulness, worldliness, self-pleasing. It is nothing but self.

Are you going to confess that tonight? My life might have been full of the Holy Ghost and full of Jesus, full of humility and full of God. But, alas, what has my life been, and all through that cursed evil root of self. I did not know how bad it was and how it was running my whole Christian life. If I could tear it out of my life and kill it, I

---

[72] Matthew 12:43-45

would do it if it cost me blood. You cannot do that. But you can do something that is better. You can come and quietly condemn it at the feet of Jesus as an accursed thing. You can cast it down there and say, "Son of God, I follow Thee with my whole heart to the very uttermost. I desire to follow Thee to the very depths of death. I desire to give myself up utterly and wholly to Thee. I desire to take Thee and let Thee fill my whole being."

Believer, Christ can do it! I know I am speaking in vain if there is any one here who is pretty well contented with himself. Anyone who says, "I am an earnest Christian, I am doing my best. I am not what I ought to be; but I do fairly." If there is any one here who thinks thus, I have not much hope of his taking this step. But if there is one who says, "I feel sinful, I feel wretched, I cannot live this life any longer. I have denied my Lord Jesus too often already by many things I have done; but now no longer. I have tried hard but have failed. I now see the root of it all. Self has been seeking to conquer its own evil works, and has only been strengthened all the time." Come, my beloved, and bring self and lay it at the feet of Jesus. Cast it into His very bosom and believe tonight that the Son of God is coming into you to be a new self, to be your very life, because He will live in you by His Holy Spirit.

Paul says, "It is no longer I but Christ that liveth in me."[73] You may not be able to explain it, but just take the words of Paul, "I live no longer but Christ liveth in me." It is no longer the old I, the old self, it is Christ. Oh, that God might give us a sight of what that means. And may God give us grace to take the step. Nothing else can give us peace or make us holy. "Lord Jesus! come in." Shall we say this? Are you willing that God search you tonight? Come then, bow your heads and begin by telling God so. And then let God shine into your hearts and let Him show you what a cursed thing this self has been in your life. Let us bow before God.

---

[73] Galatians 2:20

5. The Holy Spirit in Ephesians

We are speaking, in these lectures, of the spiritual life. I told you on Tuesday morning that it is a great thing when a man gets a vision of what the spiritual life is, and of the fact that it is for him. On Tuesday evening and yesterday morning I spoke of the two aspects of that life—the one, the mere doctrinal, from the eighth chapter of Romans; and the other, the practical, from the words, "The fruit of the Spirit is love."[74]

I wish this morning to keep that same thought before us; because I believe the more deeply we come to understand that God means us to live the life of the Holy Spirit, the more clearly we see that Scripture points to the provision God has made by which every action of the redeemed life may be through the Holy Spirit, the more convinced we shall be that God will give us this life, and the more ready we shall be to sacrifice all to enter into it. I think it may help us to take a little Bible reading on this subject this morning, from one of the Epistles, and just look at the place that the Holy Spirit takes in the Christian life as exhibited in it.

Ephesians 1:13

Turn to the Epistle to the Ephesians, Chapter 1, and the thirteenth verse. "In whom, after that ye believed, (that is, in Christ) ye were sealed with the Holy Spirit of promise." We have here first of all the sealing of the Holy Spirit.

"Believing, you were sealed." Just look at the three thousand on the day of Pentecost. They believed and were baptized and received the

---

[74] Galatians 5:22

Holy Ghost, and they were sealed with the Holy Spirit of promise. Now, you know what a seal is: the sealing of a letter or document is for safety and confirmation. God gives to His child at conversion the Holy Spirit as a seal, which is the mark of God set upon him that he may know that he is God's redeemed child. That seal is not a dead one, but is the living Holy Spirit, the Holy Spirit of promise. The Holy Spirit seals me as an earnest of my inheritance, as a spirit of promise; and when that Spirit seals me I am to trust and hope for all God is going to do.

If I am to live a healthy Christian life, I must carry the living seal of the living Spirit of God in my life every moment. I must pray to God for this living heaven-born consciousness of being the child of God, to be so clear that every moment I can realize it. The father of a family, a workman, a soldier, a sailor, every man, carries about with him the consciousness of what he is. Just so the Holy Spirit will so enable a man to realize, "I am sealed with the Holy Spirit from heaven," that He will feel, "I cannot do anything inconsistent with my position and nature." The Holy Spirit reminds me I am God's dear child.

Ephesians 1:17

The second passage you find at the 17th verse: "I cease not to give thanks for you, making mention of you in my prayers; that the God of our Lord Jesus Christ, the Father of glory, may give unto you the spirit of wisdom and revelation in the knowledge of Him; the eyes of your understanding being enlightened."[75]

Here we have the Spirit of illumination, of Divine enlightenment. After having brought them to see that they were sealed with the Holy Spirit, Paul prays for them, "Father, give them the spirit of wisdom and revelation, and enlighten the eyes of their hearts." He

---

[75] Ephesians 1:17-18

prays for them because he wants them to know the height of their calling and the glory of their inheritance and the power of Christ working in them. God has prepared for us in Christ just wonderful riches. Our calling is to be holy, to live like God's sons. Our heritage is rich and precious. The power that works in us is the resurrection power of Christ by which God raised Him and set Him at His right hand. That mighty power is working in us human beings. We do not know these things from day to day because we do not continue waiting, and asking for, and yielding to the Spirit of illumination. He would give us to see what is prepared for us every day in Christ Jesus.

This week we speak about the Holy Spirit and next week about the Lord Jesus, showing how the Spirit leads to Christ and out of Christ the Spirit comes ever more abundantly. Paul prays that the Spirit might reveal Christ fully to them, and that they might know what they have in Christ. I cannot read my Bible, I cannot lead a Christian life, unless I have the Holy Spirit as the Spirit of enlightenment. It is not a special thing, but just for the ordinary Christian life. The eyes of my heart are darkened by sin; every day I must have them illuminated by the Holy Ghost. And this I must pray for. It comes in answer to humble prayer, waiting upon God.

Ephesians 2:18

In the second chapter we have, in the 18th verse, "Through whom (Christ) we have access by one Spirit unto the Father."[76]

This is the Spirit of worship whereby we are brought nigh to God through Jesus by one Spirit. I need the Spirit if I want to pray, I need Him to worship. As a little child I used to say every day to my father, "Good morning." Every morning I need to enter into God's presence and cry "Abba Father," and dwell near to God. How can I

---

[76] Ephesians 2:18

do it? Through Christ, by the Holy Spirit. Many people speak of drawing nigh to God through the blood and through Christ. We cannot praise God too much for Christ and the blood, but that is not all, there are many who don't know what it means to draw nigh through the Holy Spirit. Where a heart is filled with the Holy Spirit, there the access and abiding in God's presence is no longer an effort but the natural spontaneous breathing of the Spirit. A man cannot live a true Christian life unless he has the Holy Spirit living in him every moment. He must know and be conscious that by the Spirit he has access through Christ unto the Father.

Ephesians 2:22

Our next step is the Spirit of fellowship. Chapter 2:22. "In whom ye also are builded together for an habitation of God through the Spirit."[77]

That is to say that each one of you is not to be built up separate from the others, but you are all built up together into "an habitation of God"—so many living stones all making up the one building. You could not have this building in which we meet if all the stones were not put upon each other and united and cemented into one solid body; this makes the house fit to live in. Just so, if the church of Christ is to be what God wants, it is to be His habitation. He is to dwell in the body, but how? We are so selfish, unloving; we have so little union with each other. How am I to have a large heart for every member of the body? The Holy Spirit will do it. If I get filled with the Holy Spirit, I will love every brother and sister and will glory in the body of Christ. Do you not feel that here the great mischief in our Christian life lies? We do not know the Holy Ghost and all He is going to do for us. We do not know that it is impossible for us to live a full Christian life unless we allow the Holy Spirit to do all His work in us; unless we accept all His

---

[77] Ephesians 2:22

blessed workings. Let us ask God to show us how indispensable it is that the Holy Ghost should triumph in us individually and collectively if we are to answer God's purpose.

Ephesians 3:5

In the third chapter, fifth verse: "The mystery of Christ, which in other ages was not made known unto the sons of men as it is now revealed unto His holy apostles and prophets by the Spirit."[78]

There you have the Spirit of inspiration. The Holy Spirit reveals to the apostles and prophets hidden divine things. In the first chapter it was the Spirit of illumination, teaching every individual what he has in Christ and what Christ can do for him. Here it is the Spirit of our practice, to whom we owe the Holy Scripture and the knowledge of the mysteries of God they give. The thoughts of God's heart are large; through the Holy Spirit He reveals to His servants the prospects of God's kingdom and enriches our hearts with wonderful thoughts of the glory of God. Look at what He says in the 9th and 10th verses: "To make all men see what is the fellowship of the mystery, which from the beginning of the world hath been hid in God, who created all things by Jesus Christ. To the intent that now unto the principalities and powers in heavenly places might be known by the church the manifold wisdom of God."[79] God is working out a wonderful purpose here in the world. If I come to some great manufacturing business, and they take me about and show me all the wonderful machinery they have, I exclaim: "What power God has given to man! What a wonderful endowment the mind of man is!" But now, to think that the Everlasting God is working out a plan, "To the intent that now unto the principalities and powers in the heavenly places might be made known by the church, the manifold wisdom of God." Let us ask for

---

[78] Ephesians 3:5
[79] Ephesians 3:9-10

the Spirit that inspired the Bible to reveal to us the wonderful glory of the mystery of God. We have the Bible, but we do not understand it unless the Holy Spirit, as our Spirit of inspiration, teach us to enter into God's blessed plan.

Ephesians 3:14-16

Verses 14-16, same chapter, another prayer of Paul, shows us the Spirit as a Spirit of strength.

This is a wonderful prayer. In the first prayer it was for light, that you might know what you have got in Christ; here, for strength, that you may receive and have Christ in you. In the first chapter it was a prayer for revelation, here it is a prayer for possession: that the Holy Spirit might strengthen and Christ dwell in you by faith and fill you unto all the fullness of God. Paul prayed to God for the Spirit of strengthening. That is the Spirit we need to have every day. I pray God to make it clear to us. If you only saw it fully, that God does not mean a child of His to live one moment without the Holy Spirit you would see how impossible it is to live rightly one moment without His unceasing operation. Yet how can God do it if I do not pray, do not long for it—to have Christ dwelling in the heart; and how can I be filled unto the fullness of God unless I believe a precious promise as to what God will do by the Spirit, like this. Plead for it, claim it, give yourself up to it.

Dear friends, I pray you take this blessed Epistle alone and pray over it step by step, and mark down all of these blessings. We have heard in the three chapters of the sealing, illumination, worship, fellowship, inspiration, and strengthening of the Spirit leading up to the fullness of God. But is that really the life I am going to live? Was this Bible written to engage or please our intellect? Was it made that ministers might have work to do, and subjects to preach sermons on? No! This Bible was written, this Epistle was written, that you, by the Holy Spirit, might live every day according to it. It means nothing unless it means that. Let us try to find out what God says about the Holy Spirit, with the resolve, I am going to claim it all; the Holy Spirit is going to live in me and make it a reality

In studying the Epistle, you will notice that it consists of two parts. The first three chapters set forth the heavenly life of the believer in Christ, you will find nothing directly practical there. It begins, "Blessed be the Father of our Lord Jesus Christ who hath blessed us with all spiritual blessings in heavenly places in Christ;"[80] these are then described in Chapter 1. Then Paul prays that God would reveal it. "God hath quickened you,"[81] "You are His workmanship."[82] In Chapter 2 and 3 it is the heavenly life of the Christian, ending with prayer and worship. The three last chapters are just the opposite. They lead from heaven to earth. The heavenly man has got to live here on earth, in the world, and in the fourth, fifth, and sixth chapters you get the most simple, practical, everyday applications to the daily life you can find. These heavenly things in connection with the Holy Spirit, His divine seal, divine illumination, divine access to God, divine fellowship bringing us into God's temple, divine inspiration of God's servants, divine strengthening in the inner man—these are all hidden spiritual blessings.

Now, let us see what we get in the second part of the Epistle.

Ephesians 4:3

There you have, in the fourth chapter, the Spirit of love. We read in the third verse, "Endeavor to keep the unity of the Spirit in the bond of peace."[83]

In going back to the first two verses, you see how necessary it is to

---

[80] Ephesians 1:3
[81] Ephesians 2:1
[82] Ephesians 2:10
[83] Ephesians 4:3

have the Spirit of love and humility as the first graces of the Christian life. Paul knew that there is no want so prevalent among men as the want of humility and of love; and so, from the heavenly heights of the previous chapters, he comes down and says, "Walk worthy of your calling as Christians, by being very humble, and being very loving; bear with one another, and do your utmost to keep the unity of the Spirit in the bond of peace."[84] How much—as I have had occasion to say before—how much there is among Christians of want of love, of want of humility; how much there is we can find in our own heart of temper, of pride, of hatred, unkindness, just coming out of that cursed flesh! "Keep the unity of the Spirit." But am I not under the power of the flesh? Am I not without the strength to keep the unity of the Spirit? The flesh cannot do the Spirit's work. I am to keep the unity of the Spirit by yielding to the Spirit. We read in Chapter 2 that He builds up believers into one body as the habitation of God. This is His work. I must have the fullness of the Holy Ghost if I am always to be living in the unity of the Spirit in the bond of peace, if I am always to be humble and loving.

Are there any of you who say, "Oh God let my life become perfect?" You must have the Holy Spirit dwelling in you every minute. I have lived for more than 60 years and have been breathing the air during all that time. I need to have fresh air every moment, I cannot live on the air I breathed 10 minutes ago, and God has provided for its being there. Just as essential as air is to your natural life, so the Holy Spirit is to a right Christian life; and if we want that, we must find out how a man may come to live every moment in the power of the Holy Spirit. It is true, I cannot be thinking about the Holy Spirit all day. But I do not think about the air either. Even as with the air, so God can keep us under the power of the Spirit all the day. As we begin to see the heavenly possibilities of an actual life in Christ Jesus, then we shall

---

[84] Ephesians 4:1-3

understand that we can indeed keep the unity of the Spirit in the bond of peace. Oh, shame upon us! What does every little finger tell you? Every little finger says, "I am at the service of the head and at the service of the body." You believe that you are a member of the body of Christ. Do be assured that the Holy Spirit will come into your life with such love and power that you will indeed keep in the unity of the Spirit, and be at the service of every member of the body. It is not enough that you keep in the unity of the doctrines of your church. Let us indeed keep the unity of the Spirit in the bond of peace! Shall we not say, "God help us?"

Ephesians 4:25-31

Then we find, further on in the fourth chapter, another very practical thing connected with the Holy Spirit. We see there He is the Spirit of holiness. In the first half of the chapter He is the Spirit of love; here He is the Spirit of holiness. Paul had been writing about a number of sins. Read from the 25th verse to the 31st. "Put away all these things" ... "they grieve the Holy Spirit of God by which ye were sealed unto the day of redemption."[85]

He is the Spirit of holiness. Saying you are not at home when you are, and excusing yourself on the ground that it is a custom of society; telling an untruth to get out of trouble; only telling a half truth or giving a false impression and say it is excusable because you did not want to hurt the feelings of others—whether it is a "black lie" or a "white lie," you grieve the Holy Spirit of God. Bitterness, clamor, and evil speaking, just telling news about others you need not tell—the facts may be true but you talk about them needlessly. This grieves the Holy Spirit. Now, don't you see how easily we grieve the Holy Spirit and the absolute necessity of being guided by the Spirit every minute? We speak about the baptism of power. We need the Holy Spirit to get into our life, to sanctify every

---

[85] Ephesians 4:25, 30

act of our being.

Ephesians 5:9

The third thing we have in the second half of the Epistle is in the fifth chapter, ninth verse: "For the fruit of the Spirit is in all goodness, and righteousness, and truth." There we have another practical thing—the fruitfulness of the Holy Spirit. What beautiful fruit the Holy Spirit brings forth! Kindness, righteousness, and truth. How can I always bring forth this fruit unless I always have the Holy Spirit within me?

Ephesians 5:18

The fourth thing, in the 18th verse of the same chapter: "Be not drunk with wine but be filled with the Spirit."[86]

Oh what a word! I cannot begin to speak about it at this time. The question is this: If I am only half or three-quarters filled with the Spirit, how can I live in the Spirit? I must have Him fill my whole nature. We must understand this. A man wants his lungs filled perfectly with the fresh air. A man with only one half his lungs can only have them partly filled and we count him diseased. When a man cannot get fresh air in a room he goes outside and opens his lungs. We must be filled with the Holy Ghost. God offers it to us. It is not a spiritual attainment, to be reached by a long process. The moment a man's whole being yields to the Spirit he can count upon being filled with the Spirit.

Paul was writing to a congregation just come out of heathenism. He had to tell some of them not to lie, or steal, etc. He wrote to them, "Brethren, do not do that which grieves the Holy Spirit, but

---

[86] Ephesians 5:18

be entirely filled with the Spirit. Obey this command and you will get right, and all the fruits of the Spirit will be manifested in you."

Ephesians 6:17

In the last chapter we have two more blessed teachings, both most precious. In the Christian life there is nothing more important than the Word and prayer. In the 17th verse we read, "Take the helmet of salvation and the sword of the Spirit, which is the word of God."[87] When the Spirit of God has filled one, he can handle the sword of the Spirit, which is the word of God, and not otherwise. This is the reason of so much preaching without fruit, because we use the sword of the Spirit without being filled with the Spirit.

The word of God is a sword in a double way. Every time I read the word of God I ought to let the word search me, and He must come like a two-edged sword dividing soul and Spirit—entering even to the very joints and marrow of the inner man. The Holy Spirit alone can do that. Then it is also the sword of the Spirit we need when fighting, not only with individual, but with national sins and unrighteousness. It is not the sword I take, but the sword the Spirit takes and uses through me. Remember, all of you who are preachers, teachers, and workers, you must be filled with the Holy Spirit. He must be in you all the time, or your use of the word will be vain. The Spirit wants to live in us every moment; then service will be the natural outcome of an indwelling life. Only let the Spirit have possession. He will use you.

Ephesians 6:18

The last we have is prayer: "Praying always with all prayer and supplication in the Spirit and watching thereunto with all

---

[87] Ephesians 6:17

perseverance and supplication for all saints."[88] The Spirit is a Spirit of prayer and supplication, and Paul stirs them up to pray continually for themselves and for all saints, and for him. Remember, friends, if there is one thing we need to be sure of, it is that God has given us the keys of the kingdom of heaven in the promises of prayer. I suppose not one earnest Christian but will be willing to confess that if he gave time enough to prayer—if he learned to use his privilege, if he would become a man of intercession—he could have done so much more for the world. How can we get that? The answer is, the Holy Spirit must fill and rule your daily life.

Now, friends, what is the application? It is very simple. First, we all want to say, "Thank God for the wonderful revelation of what the Holy Spirit can do to me." Then let us ask the Spirit of sealing to let each one know every moment that he is a child of God; the Spirit of illumination, to have the Spirit reveal Christ every minute, so that I can always know what I have in Christ; the Spirit of access to God, to lift me up to God in Christ; the Spirit of fellowship with all saints round about me; the Spirit of inspiration, revealing truths to the apostles and to us; the Spirit of strengthening, bringing from heaven the divine power through which Christ dwells in our heart by faith. These are the aspects on the heavenly side.

In the outward life, the Spirit of lowliness and love, keeping the unity of the Spirit; the Spirit of holiness, never grieving Him by a single wrong thing or thought; the Spirit of fruitfulness, bringing forth in me all kindness, righteousness; the fullness of the Spirit, so that I may expect Him to take possession of every faculty of my being, entirely filling me; the sword of the Spirit, which is the word of God, to work in me and around me; last of all, the Spirit of prayer, lifting me up into God's presence to plead for myself, to plead for the church, to plead for all sinners, to plead for those who speak, that boldness may be given unto them. Paul had been

---

[88] Ephesians 6:18

preaching for 20 years, and yet he says so earnestly. "Pray for me."
Let us pray for the ministers of the gospel.

We cannot do all this unless the Holy Spirit carries us along, unless
our whole life is full of the Spirit. Do you see, this glorious life is a
prepared, a provided life? Are you going to accept it? Say, "Oh
Lord, this is the life Thou hast promised; this is the life the Spirit
will give; I am going to be content with nothing less; I am going to
claim it. Beloved Savior, Thou hast purchased me with Thy blood,
Thou hast promised me the Spirit from the Father, I claim it."

Let us bow in prayer.

6. Be Filled with the Spirit (first lecture)
(Acts 2:4, Ephesians 5:18)

You will find the words of my text in the Acts of the Apostles, second chapter, fourth verse: "And they were all filled with the Holy Ghost." Along with that look at Ephesians 5:18: "Be filled with the Spirit." The first of these words is history: the 120 disciples were filled with the Holy Ghost. The second is a command: "Be filled with the Holy Spirit."

There are often very difficult questions suggested in connection with the question, "How can we be filled with the Spirit?" I do not think there is any better way to answer these than by looking at the disciples and seeing how they were prepared for receiving the Spirit and being filled with Him; and I know of nothing more instructive. Christ does not give the Spirit to an unprepared soul. He could not. And therefore it is of extreme consequence to ask the question, "What is needed if I am to be filled with the Spirit?"

I tried to point out from God's word this morning, as we studied the Epistle to the Ephesians in its teaching on the Spirit, that to be filled with the Spirit is what every Christian needs, and needs for his every-day life; and I repeated what I had said before, that it is not enough to look for the Spirit as a Spirit of power for work, but we ought to long above everything that our inner life be filled with the Spirit—the power for work will come out of this. If I want an apple tree to bear apples, I take care that that apple tree has as good and as strong and as healthy a growth as can be given; the apples come spontaneously. If I have the Holy Spirit strengthening and filling my inner life, the fruit of power will come.

The disciples were all filled with the Holy Spirit. Just look at the most important points in connection with their preparation: Who were they? What had they done? What had Christ done for them?

1. They were men who had forsaken all for Christ.

It was three years before this time that Christ had taken them into His school of preparation for Pentecost. John, the Baptist, said, "He will baptize you with the Holy Ghost and with fire,"[89] and when Christ called them it was with the special thought of training them for the baptism of the Holy Ghost. Missionaries often take candidates into their class for baptism for three months or a year. They come to them and say they want to be baptized. They appear earnest, but there is no satisfactory evidence that they are regenerated. The missionary says, "Come to the class; I will teach you and I will see if you are prepared to be baptized." So did Christ take these men for three years into His baptism class, and at the end of three years He baptized them with the Holy Ghost.

What was their condition on entering the baptism class? They had given up all for Christ. They had to give up their fishing nets; Matthew had to leave the receipt of the custom; they had to forsake all. Christ often repeated the truth, "Except a man hate father and mother, except a man forsake houses and lands, he is not worthy of Me."[90] On one occasion Peter said, "Lord, we have forsaken all and followed Thee."[91] My dear friends, it was this that was the first step in their preparation for the Baptism of the Spirit at Pentecost. Christ could not impart His own heavenly life and Spirit except to men who gave up all to receive Him. He took these men to prepare them and teach them to give up everything for God so they could be His disciples.

---

[89] Matthew 3:11
[90] Luke 14:26, Matthew 19:29
[91] Matthew 19:27

Jesus Christ comes to us with the same demand, "Except a man forsake all he cannot be My disciple." There are many who try to be filled with the Spirit—and it is better to try than not to try—still many try, who yet have no conception of what it is that has to be given up. I must let go the world; I must let go family and friends so far as the supreme place in my heart is concerned; I must be prepared to let go possessions, honor of men and opinions of men; I must be prepared to let go everything I have; I must be prepared to let go self, my intellect, my heart's affections, everything must be sacrificed and made subordinate to this wonderful blessing—the Holy Spirit to come and dwell in me.

The Holy Spirit is not something I can merely own or have at my disposal, but in Him Christ is a Divine Master, coming to take charge of me, and He wants every breath of my life, every word of my tongue; He wants the whole of the self-life deposed to make room for His life. Christ comes and tells me that the most important—the only—thing on earth worth living for is to be filled with the Spirit. The man who possesses Him, Christ lives in him and has complete dominion over him. He possesses Christ.

Dear friends, there are many of you who have done it, who have forsaken all for Christ. Have you not often attended a consecration meeting and taken your vow over and over again, and sung the words, "Here I give my all to Thee / Friends, and time, and earthly store."[92] and, "All I have I leave for Jesus?"[93] Have you not sung this evening, "Anywhere, everywhere with Jesus?"[94] I speak to you, who are earnest Christians, have you not forsaken all? Have you not vowed to forsake everything? Have you not vowed to forsake every selfish thing, your own pleasure, your own self, profit, and the world, and be wholly for Jesus? I tell you, you have taken the first step to be filled with the Spirit. Trust God, He will do it.

---

[92] *I Am Coming To The Cross* by William McDonald
[93] Most likely *Sad And Weary With My Longing* by B. M. Adams
[94] Most likely *Anywhere With Jesus* by Jessie Brown Pounds, Helen C. A. Dixon

If you have done it, then I want you to come under the solemn conviction, "I can be filled with the Holy Spirit, and I am going to take every step God shows me." But if there is anything in which your heart condemns you, beware! If your secret conviction is, "I have not forsaken all, there are little sins I have never given up, there is my temper, my own will, which I dare not forsake," then, I ask you, how can you expect to be filled with the Spirit? It cannot be. Oh, brother, come tonight! Do not hesitate any longer! There is the Everlasting God in heaven waiting to fill you with His holy, blessed, divine Spirit; and will you, for the sake of something in the world, or for the sake of the flesh and its pleasure, or for the sake of your own will, hold back and say, "No, I cannot be filled with the Spirit, I must give up too much"? I wish I could plead with you to come. Come! For God's sake let us all say tonight, "I forsake all to follow Jesus. I long to be filled with the Holy Ghost; I want the heavenly life to live in me fully every moment. I want to pray that I may have this pearl of great price.'

The first condition of receiving the Holy Ghost, then, was that these men had forsaken all.

And the second condition:

2. They had been brought to utter self-despair.

It was at the very beginning of Christ's teaching that He taught them to forsake their boats and fishing-nets, but later on they found they had a very difficult lesson to learn: to forsake self. We had that in the words to Peter, last night, "Let a man deny himself."[95] They did not know how terrible the power of self within them was. They were never brought to utter self-despair until they came to the cross of Jesus.

---

[95] Matthew 16:24

I cannot but remind you of the Lord's Supper. Two things took place. One was, they had a dispute among themselves as to who should be chief[96]; there was pride. They were thinking of their own glory, and of the place they would have in the new kingdom which was going to be set up. The other thing was, when Christ was led away to be crucified, they all forsook Him and fled.[97] Every one had said, "I will never forsake Thee," so self-confident were they. Peter had said, "Though all men forsake Thee yet will not I,"[98] and when Christ said, "You will deny Me," Peter said, "Though I should die with Thee yet will I not deny Thee."[99] They were filled with a self-confident spirit, and it was with that spirit that Christ took them to Gethsemane. There began the time of trial; they all fell asleep.[100] Even the three who were taken into the inner garden could not watch with Jesus. What happened then? When the soldiers bound Jesus they all forsook Him and fled. Peter and John, after a little, recovered their courage and went to the house of the High Priest, and there Peter denied his Lord. And Jesus looked upon him and he went out and wept bitterly.[101]

When Christ was condemned and taken to Calvary, there, a great distance off, they stood and looked! How their hopes perished! How they were brought to utter self-despair! Just think, when they saw their Lord crucified, and dying, and dead, and buried, what must have passed through their hearts? They had hoped for a kingdom, and all hope of the kingdom was gone forever in their eyes. They had hoped their Lord was to reign in glory, and now all was lost. Their hope was gone. Worst of all, they had trusted in themselves that they loved Jesus and would be faithful unto Him, and now they were all ashamed and hardly dared to look at each other. We have forsaken Him and fled! We never knew we were so

---

[96] Luke 22:24
[97] Matthew 26:56
[98] Matthew 26:33
[99] Matthew 26:35
[100] Matthew 26:40
[101] Matthew 26:69-75

wicked; we never knew our self was so strong and sinful. We have forsaken our beloved Lord in His hour of agony and death!

I do believe that that Sabbath day of rest was a day of unutterable anguish to those disciples, like a day of death. Why? In order that they might be broken down from all trust in anything external and anything in themselves. These two things had so broken them down that on earth there was no help, no hope at all; they were in utter despair, and thus prepared for the Holy Spirit. The Holy Spirit must come to take the place of self-life—so consuming it that a man can say, "The life that I now live in the flesh, I live by the faith of the Son of God."[102] It is only out of the grave of self that the Spirit life can rise. The Holy Spirit must work this in me. With no human help, with the hope of everything on earth broken, empty, hopeless, helpless, they turn to Christ. Why did God allow all this? That they might be empty to receive the new life, the life of the Holy Spirit. Christ came on the resurrection day to breathe upon them the Holy Spirit.[103] They then began to see something of what was coming, though during the 40 days He was with them they did not quite understand all. For what they did not understand there was nothing to do but trust. When He went back to heaven and the Holy Spirit was poured out and filled them at Pentecost, then they were fully delivered of all self-confidence.

I trust there are many here whom God has brought to the end of self. Oh, it is a blessed thing! Are there not some who say, "I want to find out whether I am prepared to be filled with the Holy Spirit?" Are you brought to utter self-despair? Perhaps many of you have asked and received what you thought was a baptism of the Holy Spirit, but you did not know the dangers. You have said, "Well, that is a wonderful thing I have got, a wonderful blessing; God has done a great thing in me;" and there was a secret self-satisfaction, and a great want of humility, and a great want of utter

---

[102] Galatians 2:20
[103] John 20:22

nothingness before God. Come and say, I want to be forever done with self; I will deny self; I have asked God to cast it out, and that my heart may be empty and broken.

That is the second step to be filled with the Holy Spirit. Get down, lower down! Do not be in a hurry to get up. My brother, get lower down, and become nothing, and let self be cast into the depths. The lowly, truly humble, self-despairing one is prepared for the baptism of the Spirit.

Are there some souls who say, "Self is still the great force in my life; self is ruling me; he is a hard master; self is working in me every day, and I have not been brought to utter self-despair?" Then I ask you, are you going to miss the blessing? Are you who are in utter self-despair about getting the blessing, are you going to try for years to improve self, to bind self with chains, to make self something not so very wicked as it is? Or will you not say, "There is no help in self; I will trust Christ to come in and take possession"? Your Father longs to have, as children, a church of believers filled with the Holy Ghost, and He has got the residue of the Spirit in great abundance. He has purposed to give it to you as He gives the water and air, freely and abundantly. The river of the water of life is flowing full from the throne of God. He wants you to say, I long to have my whole being saturated, fully dominated, ruled, possessed by the Holy Spirit of God.

Brother, if you have despaired of yourself, thank God that it is so! If you have not, are you willing here to cast self at the feet of Jesus, and to fall in utter helplessness and say, "Lord, I cannot conquer self; I have been fighting but I have failed; have mercy upon me! Let it henceforth be, None of self but all of Thee?" Come and take the place of the disciples and you will be prepared for the fullness of the Spirit.

3. They were men in whom there was an intense personal attachment to Jesus.

You know, the Holy Spirit is the Spirit that the Father gives, and He comes through the Son, Jesus Christ. He is the Spirit of God's Son, and it is by getting united to the Son of God that I get the Spirit of God.

Christ taught His disciples to cling to Him, to love Him, to delight in Him and to lean their whole weight—as it were—upon Him. In living three years with them, He had taught them to love Him. With all their failures, they did love Christ truly. There was ingratitude with it; the failures were terrible, with all the self-confidence and sins of the flesh; yet they loved Jesus. But was that enough, that they loved Jesus? No, it was not. Without the Spirit, how continually they failed to obey Christ! It was His blessed work to lead them on to a better life, where they would have power to conquer self and sin.

For over three years He walked with them as a friend. How He loved them! How He served them! How all His kindness and goodness were exhibited in their presence! Oh, how He loved them! It is written, "Having loved His own, He loved them unto the end."[104] And He had won their hearts. They loved His teaching, and they loved Him. Amid all their unfaithfulness they clung to Him. When He died, though they had gone and left Him and they believed Him dead, still they loved Him. Their hearts were attached to Him.

Here is our third step in the preparation for the baptism of the Holy Spirit. It is when the heart of a believer clings to Jesus with an intense and continual love. There are some Christians in whom there is very little personal attachment to the Lord Jesus. A man may preach sermons about Christ, talk about Him, work for Him, and give liberally, but this is not what I am speaking about. What was the charge of Christ against the church at Ephesus? "Thou hast

---

[104] John 13:1

left thy first love."[105] There was no personal tender love to Jesus.

There are some people who talk about being filled with the Spirit, and pray for it, but I am afraid they will not get it. They do not know what it is to be clinging to Jesus as a personal friend. Before the soul is filled with the Spirit there is a tenderness of feeling, a preparation for it in the intensity of love for Jesus; there is a clinging of the heart to Himself; the soul is longing for Him, and longing to love Him better. There are some of you, I trust, who can say, "I do love Jesus; He knows how I delight in Him; He knows that He is the joy of my heart, and tonight He knows that I burn for Him; He knows I ask, 'What can I sacrifice for my Lord Jesus? Is there anything I can do for Jesus?' He knows that, amid failure, I am seeking to keep every commandment, and my heart's prayer is, 'Oh, that I could see Him and know Him better! Oh, for the time when God has all my heart; and nothing there but Jesus, Jesus only.'"

Praise God for every soul that is broken, who says in faith towards God, "Lord, Thou knowest all things, Thou knowest that I love Thee."[106] Take courage! Say it with boldness, as Peter did, or say it sorrowing; but say it! You are in the right path to be baptized with the Holy Spirit. Jesus wants people who are intensely full of love to Him.

We often hear the complaint, "My religion is more in my head, and in my work, than in intense love to Jesus." O, Lamb of God, who loved us! We see we have been so busy with ourselves, with our study, our preaching, our visiting, our working for Thee—so busy with these that for Thee, blessed Lamb of God, we have had little time, so little time for meeting with Thee; so little heart and longing for close union!

---

[105] Revelation 2:4
[106] John 21:17

Let us fall down and make confession, "Lord, Thou canst not give me the Holy Spirit; I am wanting this mark; I have so little love. Oh, tell me, when can I get it? How long must I seek this love?" You can get it to-night if you see your sin and shame, and confess the want of this personal, clinging love, and say, "Lord, let my love now be a tender, intimate fellowship; I want my whole being to be filled with the love of God." Say it in humility and say it in faith. He accepts that, when the soul has pledged itself to begin loving Him wholly. He will accept it, and will send down His Holy Spirit upon you. Sister, brother, are you ready? Jesus wants to fill us with His Holy Spirit.

4. They had accepted the word of Christ about the coming of the Spirit, in faith.

They were men who believed. Those ten days after Christ's Ascension were passed in waiting and prayer. That is faith. What did they believe about it? Ask them. They could not tell exactly. They had read in the Old Testament of the Holy Spirit coming down on prophets; but about the Holy Spirit dwelling in the believer all day, and the Holy Spirit bringing the joy and presence of Jesus into their hearts, they did not know. They just believed. Our master said that He would send the Holy Spirit[107]; they just clung to that word. He said it, and we are sure of it.

"How foolish to think of the Holy Spirit coming from heaven for the sake of people like you!" someone might exclaim. Their answer is: "He said it." If people had said, "You fools! you denied Him, you forsook Him, you unworthy creatures! Do you believe you are going to be the elect men?" They would answer, "He said it."

Now are you resting upon the word of God? This morning we had the picture of the wonderful life that the child of God can live, all

---

[107] Luke 24:49

those twelve aspects of the walk in the power of the blessed Spirit. That is what the Bible says can be my life. Some of you were here when we spoke about the fruit of the Spirit being love. Have not all of you said, "I believe that my life can be a life of love all the day long—love to the most unlovable, to the heathen, love to all I meet?" Have you said that in faith? Have you said, "The Holy Spirit can be in my soul; I can be filled with the Holy Spirit"? Can you say, "I can have the filling every morning and night"? Oh, take care! Don't let unbelief tell you that this is too high for a man on earth, that a man in the flesh cannot live filled with the Spirit. That is unbelief.

Another says, "My temperament! There are people who have a kind temperament; but, you know, I have such a temperament, I could never have this fullness." And so on, in a hundred forms there is the thought, "We must be content to live without the Spirit." Beloved children of God, take care of unbelief, and come now tonight and say, "I do believe what Jesus says: that the Father delights to fill a child of His with the Holy Spirit. I do believe that the life of the Holy Spirit is meant to be lived by me every day in the week and every moment of my life. I do believe what the Scriptures say, that the Holy Spirit is able to fill me with God's love, so that my life shall be one of humility and tenderness, giving glory to God and the Lord Jesus."

If you will believe what God has said, and what God is willing and waiting to do by the power of the Holy Spirit, though you don't feel it yet, say that you believe it. If you believe there is a God in heaven, and there is a blessing waiting, and God is willing to give it, will you say that? It is an unutterably solemn thing to come into contact with God. A man must stand and give an answer to God. Many turn round to think about it, and will not give an answer to God. Oh, come and do something! Set your heart upon it and say, I will have it!

Some are thinking of their business and how it would look for them to go down tomorrow morning if they were overflowing with the Holy Spirit. Just imagine it! They think: "I cannot do it; I could not manage it!" You have not to manage the Holy Spirit; He will manage you. He will teach you how to live when you are full of Him.

5. They not only believed, but they longed and thirsted for it.

I believe that, with the shock of that earthquake that came to them when Jesus was crucified, in their utter despair of themselves and with inexpressible shame and disgrace for having treated Jesus as they did, they learned to long for something better. And the Son of God, in the 40 days He was upon the earth, worked in their hearts an expectation that filled them with assurance during the 10 days in which they waited. These 120 men and women appeared contemptible in the eyes of the world, but they waited for the promise of their Lord. They were assured of this above everything.

Are you willing to do this? May God bring us to it! It struck me as a solemn thing. This is the last evening service this week, and how far have we got? Friend, would you be ready to say, "God, fill me with the Holy Ghost; I am ready." Are you ready to say that?

Some people think it must come as a great emotion, stirring their whole being. It does not always come that way. It may come as the night-dew on the grass, quiet and gentle. They think people must talk and shout. No! What is it? It is to have my whole being placed at His disposal, and then in faith to receive the gift of God; the Holy Spirit taking possession of me; as an empty vessel to separate myself to be filled with the Holy Spirit, and believe then: the Lord has given this life, to be filled with the Holy Spirit. I claim it from Him! I trust Him for it!

You know, a river can be filled in two ways. In South Africa we have terrible valleys, which might be called dry rivers, and then high up the course of the river there come immense thunder storms and the water comes pouring down with such a rush that it causes the stream in these lower reaches to rise eight or ten feet high at once, and it keeps on rising until it overflows its banks. How did it get full? Suddenly, with violence. But sometimes rivers get full in quite a different way. There are great snow mountains, and the show melts gently, and the water flows and fills the river. There is very little commotion. The stream rises slowly, and gradually the river gets full, until its banks overflow. How different from the former!

There are souls in whom the filling of the Holy Ghost comes with great emotion. There are other souls who come trembling, and full of fear. They are prepared and they say to God, "O God, it is Thy will that I should be filled with the Holy Spirit from morning to night. I long for it. I believe Thou wilt give it." They say it quietly and they claim it in faith. "Lord, I believe Thou hast done it."

Oh, my brother, are you ready for it tonight? Remember, the Holy Spirit is the heritage of God's Church. It is not meant for something extraordinary. Each of us may say, "The fullness of the Holy Spirit is mine. It is mine for my daily life, to enable me to live a holy life every day."

Are you ready? Shall we bow before God?

7. Praying in the Power of the Holy Ghost
(Romans 8:22-27)

I want to speak to you this morning on prayer. Those of you who are students preparing for the work of making known the gospel of Christ can hardly realize the part prayer ought to play in your studies. People think a great deal of study. They study Latin, Greek, logic and science of all sorts. They will study music and theology and anything that will help them in the work of the ministry or in service of the gospel, and yet very often forget what is the—it is a solemn thing to say—what is the most important part of the preparation for the work of serving God. That is prayer! And prayer is an art, a spiritual art that has to be studied like anything else.

You know we don't become perfect in anything without a great deal of exercise. When a person is learning to play the piano he spends—it may be an hour every day, sometimes many hours—all for the sake of being perfect in his art. Do not let us think we can learn the art of prayer without a great deal of exercise. Just think what its importance is in preaching, in visiting, in speaking, in dealing with men, when God's word tells me that all my dealing is helpless except God's power from heaven works. And the word tells me that the power will work in answer to the much prayer of faith, praying with importunity, and that alone. "Paul may plant, Apollos water, but God giveth the increase."[108]

Someone has said that farmers are a people who ought to learn to trust God. They can sow their corn, but they must wait on God to give sunshine or rain for growth and increase. This is specially true

---

[108] 1 Corinthians 3:6

for people who are going to work for God. I may plow, I may sow, I may work as hard as man can work, but God gives the increase. And God gives the increase in answer to prayer. And so for two reasons, dear students, you all ought to be men and women of prayer. One reason is for your own spiritual life. If the Holy Spirit is to live in your life it must come by prayer. The other is for the sake of those among whom you work. If the Holy Ghost is to work in them through the word it must come by prayer. And do not think after I become a minister, missionary, or teacher, then I will begin to pray, then I will learn to pray because I shall then feel the need. You say, "I cannot find time to pray now. I have so many lessons to prepare I need every moment for study, I cannot be behind in my class, I cannot give time to prayer." Oh, beware! Remember the same devil that teaches you this now will find you three years hence when your work is much heavier. He will tell you the same; that you have so much to do that you cannot find time to pray. Remember, the unconverted man says, conversion is easy to-morrow but hard to-day. Even so prayer that now is difficult, appears easy in the future. Alas, you will find it in the future just as hard as now.

I pray that you students preparing for Christ's work ask God to teach you how to pray. He cannot do that unless you give time to it. Reading a book about prayer, listening to lectures and talking about it is very good, but it won't teach you to pray. You get nothing without exercise—without practice. I might listen to a professor of music for a year playing the most beautiful music, but that won't teach me to play. So take care that you don't get beautiful thoughts about prayer; take care that you don't get beautiful Scripture truths about prayer and yet don't put them into practice by actually praying.

The words that I want to speak on will put prayer before us in a wonderful way. It stands connected with the work of the Holy Ghost. They are found in the eighth chapter of Romans, 23rd verse. Let us read from the 22nd verse:

*"For we know that the whole creation groaneth
and travaileth in pain together until now."*

Paul says, throughout creation there is a groan of suffering and crying for deliverance to God and not only this creation is groaning but, "We ourselves which have the first fruits of the Spirit, groan within ourselves waiting for the adoption, to wit: the redemption of the body."[109] And also verses 26 and 27. Now in these two last verses I have read I think you will find four precious thoughts about prayer:

1. We are ignorant and do not know how to pray

2. The Holy Spirit is our helper in prayer

3. The Holy Spirit prays for us not always in words or thoughts that we can understand, but with unutterable groanings, longings that cannot be expressed

4. That God who searches the heart finds out what the mind of the Spirit is who always prays according to God's will and God gives us the answer

In the first place,

1. We are ignorant and know not how to pray.

When I have got to do a thing and I am ignorant, it is of great importance that I should know my ignorance. If I were to ask a teacher of music to teach me to play on the piano and I sat down with the idea that I could do it, it would hinder him terribly. But if I sat down in my ignorance and said, "Please teach me how, then I am in the right position to be taught." So there are a great many who have the idea that they can pray. They say, "Our mother taught us to pray, our minister taught us to pray. I know of many things I

---

[109] Romans 8:23

have gotten from God." They think everyone can pray. How often we think we know how to pray, and go on for years with the idea we are praying right.

Now, if you are ever to become powerful in prayer, the first thing in prayer must be that you fall down before God, under a sense of your ignorance, and say, "I cannot pray as I ought." Ere you begin to pray just quietly say, "Do I know what prayer is? Do I know what it is to meet the great God? Do I know how to take hold of God and hold Him fast? Do I know how to take hold of His strength? Do I know what the full fellowship and communion of God is?" Begin to sit still until you realize His holy presence and feel how little you are fit to speak to Him. "Lord, I know not how to pray. I may know many things to pray for but not what I need most."

My prayer may be right—"Lord deliver me from pride and self-will"—and yet I may not know how sadly I need pride to be removed. Perhaps God wants me to be delivered from pride and I pray for that, and yet I have never seen myself as God sees me—I have never been truly convicted of my pride. So you can pray for other things and never come to the real point of what you need. You need before everything in prayer a deep consciousness of your ignorance. What a wonderful blessing if I come into this ignorance. The Holy Spirit will be my helper in prayer.

This blessed ignorance is one of the most remarkable elements of faith. Abraham went out not knowing whither he went. It was a beautiful ignorance, it taught him to trust God. Look at the disciples. They once came to ask Jesus to give them a place on the throne. He said, "Ye know not what ye ask."[110] He brought them at once to the point. You think you are asking for what you need. No! You are foolish. You know not what you ask.

Very often we pray for the baptism of the Holy Spirit and we don't

---

[110] Matthew 20:22

know what we are praying for. It is of the utmost importance that you know what you are praying for. I may utter thoughts that are true and yet my heart may not know what I ask. So, from the very beginning there should be in our prayers a sense of deep ignorance. Paul says, "No man knoweth the things of God but the Spirit of God."[111] None of you can tell what I am thinking about. You do not know what is in my heart. No one can tell what is in the mind of God but the Spirit of God. If I come and pray from what I have learned out of a book or out of my experience, that is not enough. I want to be taught by the Spirit of God to pray as I ought, in unison with the will of God.

Oh listen, the Holy Spirit cannot teach you until all your self-conceit and self-confidence is taken away and you get broken down into a nothingness that says, "Lord, I know nothing." Thus will you learn to be quiet before God, and in your ignorance to wait on God to teach you.

2. The Holy Spirit is our helper in prayer.

What a blessed thought that the Holy Spirit is given to help our infirmities, and that He prays in us. What a blessed thought! You are believers in the Holy Trinity—Father, Son and Holy Ghost. The Father, He sits upon the throne as God. The Son sits on His right hand as Mediator and Intercessor, He lives ever to pray. Think of that! The Son in His glory has got no other work but praying. His whole being, His presence before God as the Lamb that was slain, is one unceasing prayer; and we read that that is the reason He can save completely, because "He ever liveth to pray."[112]

He is the King in glory, but His highest work is prayer, and continually there goes up to the Father from Him a stream of

[111] 1 Corinthians 2:11
[112] Hebrews 7:25

intercession: Father, bless Thy children, bless My people on earth. And unceasingly there comes from the Father in answer a stream of blessing. And unceasingly from the Son there streams out the flow of the Holy Spirit to bring the blessing to us. And the Spirit is in the heart of the believer to teach what this blessing is that Christ has for them; to teach them all that is prepared for them. But when we are self-satisfied, and imagine that we know how to pray, then we cannot wait for the Holy Spirit to teach us and we lose all the wonderful gifts He could reveal to us.

Just think what it means! The Father on the throne to give; the Son at His right hand to bless, and down in your heart and mine the Holy Spirit, the third person of the Blessed Trinity, proceeding from the Father. It is God giving, Christ praying, and the Holy Spirit receiving and imparting; teaching you to pray in perfect harmony with God and Christ. Have we actually believed, "I have the Holy Spirit to help my infirmities in prayer"? Alas! No.

When we have felt our ignorance, felt we don't know how to pray, we have begun mourning and have become discouraged; we have kept away from our closet because we did not know how to pray as we wished. I tell you, brother, that is the very best time to go and pray. When you pray so glibly and easily, it is very much human feeling and human words, and the power of the Holy Ghost is not there. When you feel you cannot pray, set yourself before God and say, "I cannot pray, prayer is too high for me, let the Holy Spirit help my infirmities and come and pray in me."

What a blessed truth it is the Holy Spirit prays in me and for me. He it is of whom we heard yesterday and the day before, that the Holy Spirit takes charge of our whole life and dwells in our hearts. If you will only take time to use your Heavenly Helper, He will do His work effectively. If I have a helper in any work—for example, in leading the singing this morning I have a helper in Professor Towner—what do I do? When it is time for singing, I give up to him and trust him for the music in the meeting. To this Holy Spirit—if

He is to be my helper—I must give way, I must stand aside.

How little we have acknowledged that the Holy Spirit has helped our infirmities. If you are to get the help of the Spirit let me give you one lesson, and let me urge this upon you: when you are in your closet to pray alone you should always take plenty of silent time before your prayers and in between your prayers. It is a solemn thing to think that I am going to exercise power on heaven and bring down here heavenly blessings upon myself and others, and I ought to be very quiet before God. Think of God, the Three-One God, as engaged in your prayer. Let us always spend a few minutes, at least, in worship, until our faith realizes, "Here is the Almighty God, waiting to bless me. He is longing to fill me with His Holy Spirit." This faith will not come unless we take time to think about it. The Everlasting God is waiting to bless me. Let me believe God will bless. Just be quiet and sink down into nothingness and let the Holy Spirit pray in you. The Holy Spirit will do it. The Father has given you His Spirit on purpose to do it. He will pray in you.

Again, when you have prayed, be quiet a little and just sit still until your heart gets fully into the faith that the Holy Spirit is doing His work in you just now. He is given to you actually and really to be your teacher and helper in prayer. When you feel very ignorant and helpless, pray! A lady once asked a minister for help. She had lost the joy of secret prayer. She asked what she had to do to get it back. She had done her best in striving but had failed. He said, "You went the wrong way about it. When you were unconverted you tried to do everything right and did not succeed. How did you get life?" "I just trusted Jesus," she said. "That's what you have got to do again. When you have no inclination to pray, when your heart is very cold, just go to Jesus and say, 'Thou hast ap pointed prayer as the means to come to Thee, and my heart is cold. Thy heart is full of love, here I come in my feebleness.' If you will abide in His presence, He will meet you, and the Spirit will teach you to trust and to pray." The Holy Spirit is given to help our infirmities.

We must take care of making a mistake. People often think that when the Holy Spirit comes and teaches them to pray, there will be a great, burning rush of feeling and they will pray such beautiful prayers. Feeling may indeed stir and help you, but many times it is superficial. Let me read the words of the text again, "But the Spirit maketh intercession for us with groanings that cannot be uttered!"[113] That is what the Spirit loves to do. He loves to keep us in our ignorance, so that our mind cannot run away and occupy itself with the beautiful thoughts from the Holy Spirit. He goes deeper than our thoughts and minds into the heart and He prays there with groanings, with longings that cannot be expressed in words. He gives us a deep, an inexpressible yearning, a deep thirst for God and for God's glory.

Oh, my friends, we are proud of nothing so much as our minds, our intellects, and our thoughts. We want to understand everything, and to know everything. You listen to a sermon and get a beautiful thought, you tell your friends of it, you keep it to read over again. You have got something for your intellect, but it has not got into your heart. A blind man can understand talk about the sun, and light, and know a great deal about it; the most ignorant man who has seen the sun knows more. A great many people know a great deal about prayer, but it does not help them to pray. We want our hearts filled with the Holy Spirit and He will bring us into the life of prayer. If the Holy Spirit alone can teach us to pray, have we not reason to confess that we have often prayed in the flesh?

Oh, may the Blessed Teacher, Himself, live and breathe in us, that we may know how to pray. May the Holy Spirit, about whom we have been speaking and thinking these last few days, be to us a Spirit of prayer, as He is in us a Spirit of holiness and of power for work; the Spirit of love, and the Spirit that brings to us all that we had yesterday morning in the Epistle to the Romans. A Spirit of fellowship, of access to God, a Spirit of intercession, who give us

---

[113] Romans 8:26

boldness and power with God.

3. The Holy Spirit makes intercession in us. He prays in and for us
in words and feelings that are as unutterable groanings.

After Paul speaks of Him as the Spirit of intercession for all saints,
he says He makes intercession for the saints according to the will of
God. What that means, we can understand if we look at the 23rd
verse: "For the whole creation groaneth." All the suffering animals
throughout the world—all the millions of little creatures around
us—these are all groaning for a different state of things. And not
only so, but we ourselves groan within ourselves, though we have
the first fruits of the Spirit waiting for the adoption, to wit: the
redemption of the body. Paul says, believers should look forward to
the full redemption, when the body shall be redeemed and made
like Christ's glorious body, and all believers gathered into one.
Creation groans for its universal redemption; the Spirit groats not
only for the individual but the united redemption of all saints.
There is a great groaning in creation and a great groaning by the
Holy Spirit in the hearts of believers, and these are things we
cannot pray for as we ought, but God hears the unutterable
groanings of the Holy Spirit. The Spirit makes intercession in us
for all saints.

It is your highest privilege as priests of God to be intercessors. Oh,
the value of the intercession! When I pray for other people who
may be at a distance, or when we gather in a small prayer-meeting,
I sometimes say, what utter folly this would be if God's word did
not teach it. Here are 50 people praying for something in China, or
Africa, or England, and these 50 feeble ones believe that they can
actually stir the Almighty Everlasting God to action by their
prayers, and that in answer to their prayers He would do
something that He would not have done if they had not prayed.
This can only be true because the Holy Spirit dwells in the believer,
and His prayer in us is from God as much as the answer.

Children of God, yield yourselves up to the Holy Spirit as the Spirit of intercession! Study your work of intercession! If all believers were only to give an hour a day for interceding for the church of God! Oh, pray for the church of God! If you would have your eyes opened, think of the state of Christendom. Take London with its five million: only one million of these go to church—four millions who practically are not Christians. Think of Chicago with one million and a half and you have only 200,000 people going to church. Just imagine! Think of those who do go to church. Out of these how many go through mere formality; how many who are living in sin; how many who are not converted, and how many who are worldly? Think that this is not only true of London and Chicago, but of all the world.

Upon you and me God has left the responsibility of praying and taking hold of Him. He has told us not to let Him go and has given us wonderful promises. Take time to pray. If we will give up ourselves to intercession, God will bless. I would like to ask everyone here, do you pray for the church of Christ in the United States? You talk about its worldliness, so much higher criticism and error. You talk about these, but do you go to God and cry, "Lord, visit Thy church?" Oh, do cry to Him, "Lord strengthen all Thy people who are trying to live true to Thee." It is one Spirit and one body and if you will give way to the Holy Spirit He will teach you to pray for the church.

Paul says to the Ephesians, "Praying always with all prayer and supplication in the Spirit, and watching thereunto with all perseverance and supplication for all saints; and for me, that utterance may be given unto me."[114] The Holy Spirit is not a selfish Spirit. The fruit of the Spirit is love and it is one Spirit and one body. May God make you young men and women—may God make all of us, men and women of intercession—filled with the power of the Holy Spirit, for this our highest and holiest work, to intercede for all saints.

4. That God who searches the heart finds out what the mind of the Spirit is who always prays according to God's will and God gives us the answer.

Last, we have the wonderful promise at the end of the verse. "He that searcheth the hearts knoweth what is the mind of the Spirit because He maketh intercession for the saints according to the will of God."[115] Just think of that. God is to come and search out our hearts. But have we not said in words what we want. Yes, but God is not deceived with words. God knows that the earnest Christian often prays in earnest words, and his heart does not truly and fully will what he has said, or, at the bottom of his heart there may be needs he has not expressed. God goes deep into the heart and finds out what the Holy Spirit says. The mind of the Spirit prays according to the will of God.

My beloved friends, it is a solemn thing to pray. I do beseech you: take time to practice prayer and in your prayer every time learn more and more to yield yourself up to the Holy Spirit and say to Him that you set the very depths of your heart open to Him. If your inmost being is humbly and patiently made subject to Him, He can take and make you, not a prayer machine, but a vessel in which He lives and in which He works His prayers down into your desires and will, so that you pray in the Spirit and the Spirit prays in you. May all of us learn the blessed privilege of intercession in the power of the Holy Ghost. May all of us know the joy of having God search our hearts and answering us abundantly according to what He finds there of the need of the Spirit. May all of us know what it is to cry to God with unutterable and unceasing longings "for all saints," that He might indeed visit and revive His people.

[114] Ephesians 6:18
[115] Romans 8:27

8. The Holy Spirit in Galatians

I want to take another Bible reading in regard to the work of the Holy Spirit. We have now looked at it from various sides. Yesterday morning we had the thoughts of God's work in the Epistle to the Ephesians. This morning I want you to take the Epistle to the Galatians and see what is taught there about the work of the Spirit. We are going to study that Epistle, not with a view to get doctrine or theology, as it is sometimes called, but we want to get teaching in regard to the Spiritual life and our daily walk.

You know that the Galatians had been converted under the preaching of Paul. There had been very blessed times, and the Holy Spirit had been among them in great power, and yet, strange to say, they had very shortly after wards gone back. They had been led away by Jewish teachers and had fallen away from the simple life of faith. Paul writes the Epistle to reprove and instruct them.

From what I have said you will see the state of the church was very low. The works of the flesh were very manifest. There was a great deal of bitterness, jealousy and clamor, consequently the teaching of the Epistle is one of warning. I wish to point out specially, how, in connection with the mention of the Holy Spirit there are certain dangers against which we need to be warned.

There are many people who think that when a man is filled with the Spirit, he is in a state of perfection. They will very soon find out that they are wrong. I want to impress this very much upon you, that when a man gets the fullness of the Spirit—the life of the Spirit—it is a thing that makes him very gentle, very humble, very much afraid of sinning against God and very tender lest he should be led to walk astray. He has a spirit of deep, deep humility and fear of pride.

Let us find out what God's word tells us and warns us to beware of.

Galatians 3:2

The first mention of the Spirit is Galatians 3:2. "This only would I learn of you, Received ye the Spirit by the works of the law, or by the hearing of faith?" There we see plainly that there are two ways in which men often think they can get the Holy Spirit.

One is by the work of the law. That is the religion of human nature. We think we must work. We have been doing wrong, of course we must do right; we have been sinning, of course we must give up sin; and the more we give up sin and obey God the more we get of the Holy Spirit. The Epistle teaches us that this is wrong. "Was it by the works of the law, or by the hearing of faith?" Did you find yourselves getting so good, so righteous, that you could say, "Now, Lord give us the Holy Spirit?" Did the Holy Spirit come upon you, in response to such a life, under the law? Or, when you were under the law, did it not show you that you were sinners, and did you not come in faith, by the obedience of faith, first accepting Jesus Christ, and then giving yourself up to obey Him fully? "By the hearing of faith" you got the Holy Spirit.

Take care, those of you who are seeking for the Holy Ghost, that you don't seek by the works of the law instead of the hearing of faith. It is a free gift of the everlasting God. It is not what you do or what you are that will get the Holy Spirit. As a condition, you have to confess sin, and to give up sin; but the more earnest and intense your desire, the more you fail, until you see that you cannot conquer sin yourself. It is as you come to Jesus and confess you are not strong enough to cast out sin, and say, "Lord, in Thy power I will live a holy life," that you will obtain the Holy Spirit. You receive the Spirit by faith.

As we read in the 14th verse of the same chapter, "That we might receive the promise of the Spirit, through faith."[116] Now remember, everyone who is beginning to long for the filling of the Holy Spirit, that here is the great truth you need, you must get it by faith. Faith always means this: there is something I cannot do myself, I trust another to do it for me. Faith is always a confession of helplessness. Faith, if it means anything, means this: "Lord, I cannot make myself worthy, but I can trust in Thy love. Thou canst and will give me the Holy Spirit. I want you to say that without any doubt." And it is not only by faith once for all, but it is by faith every morning, that the action of the Holy Spirit may be received fresh from heaven.

Many people have a precious experience and live on that for forty years. We need the Holy Spirit fresh from heaven every day. I don't know of a more solemn lesson than that of the manna that came from heaven.[117] It became corrupt twenty-four hours after it fell. Water you want every day fresh from the spring; stagnant water corrupts. If you want to live the life of the Holy Spirit, it must be a life continually renewed from heaven. I must come every day to be filled fresh with the Holy Spirit. This must be the holy habit of my life. As you began so continue, by faith. You must learn to get hold of God's promises, to believe in the divine, God-given power working in you and then your walk will be a humble one, from hour to hour. Just as a father gives bread every day to his child, so my Father gives me the blessed power of the Holy Spirit fresh every day.

The great mark of a man who lives in the Spirit is deep, true, entire, unbroken dependence upon God. As I need the sunshine every minute of the day—the sunshine of five minutes ago does not help me now; every minute the sun must shine on me from above—so every moment the Holy Spirit must come to my heart fresh from

---

[116] Galatians 3:14
[117] Exodus 16

God. And thus you receive, not by the works of the law but by the hearing of faith.

Galatians 3:4

Warning in the fourth verse. "Are ye so foolish, having begun in the Spirit are ye now made perfect in the flesh?"[118] This is a most important and instructive lesson, conveying the solemn warning, that a man can begin in the Spirit and then get off the line and go on to perfect in the flesh what was begun in the Spirit.

You know what shunting is. On a dark night a train may be switched over to another track and go off in a wrong direction. A man may receive the Holy Spirit and get shunted off the track just by one thing: the flesh. In Romans, eighth chapter, we saw the great contrast between the Spirit and the flesh. "Not in the flesh but in the Spirit," "Not after the flesh but after the Spirit." So, too, in Galatians the contrast is pressed. A man can begin with the Holy Spirit and unconsciously be led to perfect—to seek his religious progress—in the flesh.

Thousands have done it. A man has, for a time, been under the power of the Spirit, and yet been led to seek the maintenance of his life and work in what is human and carnal. You may have the Holy Spirit in you and yet you have the flesh in you too, and the flesh is always active and ready to live the religious life. I have seen men in whom the power of the Holy Ghost is manifest, and yet there is just a little of self. God uses such a man, and yet self-confidence may corrupt all. The man perfects in the flesh what was begun in the Spirit. This is a danger to which you and I are exposed and therefore we must take the warning. How can we provide against it? You cannot provide against it. Nothing on earth can bring us relief.

---

[118] Galatians 3:4

Oh, that we might have a real sense of our danger, a sense of our utter inability to keep away the secret, insidious power of the flesh! You need to pour impotence in the very depths of your being, so that you, through God, praise God that your heart is full of the joy of the Holy Ghost. You still are conscious that all the time you are in the enemies' territory and may be led to allow the flesh to assert itself in your religion. You want to be brought to such a sense of your helplessness and dependence upon God as shall lead you really to yield yourself to the Holy Spirit alone.

Dear Christians, you have a great many enemies, but watch specially against one. That one, how hard to be overthrown! It is self. Self is the flesh and the flesh is self. This is the one enemy you are in danger of allowing to come in between you and the Holy Spirit and leading you off, shunting you off on the wrong track. Beware! To those who are seeking earnestly to live lives filled with the Holy Spirit, let me say, take up a position of deep fear and dependence. God's word says, "Fear not. Look to God, be not afraid." But on the other hand, it says, "Blessed is the man who feareth."[119] The man who fears lest he should sin against God and give way to the flesh is the man who gets to fear nothing because God is his strength.

Having begun in the Spirit take care lest you perfect in the flesh.

Galatians 4:6-7

In the fourth chapter, sixth and seventh verses. "And because ye are sons God hath sent forth the Spirit of His Son into your hearts, crying, Abba, Father. Wherefore thou art no more a servant, but a son; and if a son, then an heir of God through Christ."

In the previous verse there was a warning against the spirit of

---

[119] e.g. Psalm 112

bondage, here we are taught that the Spirit that comes in us is the Spirit of adoption; we are the heirs of God in His Son. The whole teaching of the epistle is this: not to go to God as servants but as sons. You have the Spirit of sonship. You all know the parable of the prodigal son and the elder son. How the elder son said to the father, "I have served thee these many years, yet thou never gavest me a kid."[120] The father replied, "Son, thou art ever with me and all I have is thine."[121] Thou hast free access to my presence and all my possessions. What was wrong with that young man? He had the spirit of a servant and not of a son. Instead of trusting his father he was living the life of a slave.

The spirit of bondage is so natural to us. Therefore, God's word says, do remember you are sons. Let us show it in our whole lives, in our intercourse with God and our walk before men, that the spirit of a son is in us, the Spirit of God's own Son. God holds back no good thing from His sons. Our whole life ought to be in the faith, I am always a son of God. I have always everything I need. Most Christians do not enjoy that because they do not live in the spirit of sonship. The object of the Holy Spirit is to give you a full childlike heart toward God.

Here in Galatians we are warned to take care that we don't live before God as servants in the spirit of bondage. God gave the Spirit of His Son; He sent Him forth into our hearts. Oh, that we might realize the simplicity of being a child of God all the day long! My father loves me so. See the little child's actions toward his father. He loves him and jumps on his knee and says, "Won't you give me this?" The heart of the child is full of confidence in the father. How blessed if we allowed this Spirit of sonship to possess us!

Some people ask for the Holy Spirit and have somewhat of His power but their work is a burden. Allow the Spirit of God's Son,

---

[120] Luke 15:29
[121] Luke 15:31

who dwells in your heart from day to day, to deliver you from the spirit of bondage and fear—that wrong fear of a slave toward God—and give you a spirit of childlike access and openness and confidence and love.

God has sent forth the Spirit of His son into your hearts. Do not live like servants, but like sons.

Galatians 5:1-5

You see here that there were many of the Galatians, who had been justified by faith in Christ, who had taken to works again. They were seeking for obedience in an external religion, a religion of works. Beware of that. A true believer waits through the Spirit for the hope of righteousness through faith. Everything that is promised to the righteous I am to hope for. Everything I hope for, the Holy Spirit teaches me to expect by faith.

Do you not see our whole life is to be believing? Some people ask, have you not told us to work very hard? Yes, but it is a very different thing to work under the law and to work by grace. There is a law that you may not steal. How many thousands cannot keep from stealing? The law cannot put into their hearts that which shall prevent them from stealing. The law is helpless. It can punish but it cannot affect a man's heart. But faith can. There is no power in the world like faith. Thousands have been attracted to South Africa by the faith of what they heard about gold to be found there. Faith is the one power that made them leave home. Faith is the one power of the Christian life.

We are always in danger of seeking something by the works of the law. We are always in danger of thinking we ought to be doing something, instead of going to Christ, in faith, and saying, "I can do nothing, work Thou in me." That is what Paul says, "I am nothing behind the chiefest of the apostles, though I am nothing."[122] We, through the Spirit, wait for the hope of righteousness, for all the thousands of blessings that are to come to us every day of our lives. Paul teaches it in every possible way, that we must live and work in the Spirit coming from God and filling our life.

Let there, every day of your lives—every morning, especially—be a time set apart for acting faith—for exercising yourself in believing, before you pray. There are Christians who study their Bibles so earnestly for half an hour, they have read and thought on God's word, have prayed and told God what they want, but they have done no believing. They have never asked, "Do I know, certainly, that God is blessing? So I believe for certain that God is going to keep me? Am I perfectly sure God is going to guide me?" If you asked them if they believed that, they would hesitate to answer.

Take warning, and learn to say, every time you go to pray, "I am not going to pray unless I believe God is listening." Am I sure that God hears me and can I trust Him fully that He is going to bless me? Hold still a little and say, "Oh God, Thou wilt bless Thy child." If you do not feel that you can say that, all the more reason you should say, "What is wrong?" Let your heart go up in confession and tell God you are willing to give up everything; you will learn to see the teaching about the Holy Spirit and to believe in the reality of the work in you. The Holy Spirit is not merely for speaking or preaching, but for every hour of the day. Whether I eat or drink I need to have the Holy Spirit. I need to have the Holy Spirit to rule my disposition and keep me gentle, heavenly, Christlike, devoted to God.

You can never influence the church of Christ with your prayer unless the Holy Spirit is leading you. You cannot be living a holy life and a blessed life except in the full power of the Holy Ghost. What did God give the Holy Spirit for? That we might live like

---

[122] 2 Corinthians 2:11

Jesus. That our life, like His, might be the exhibition of what the power of God's Spirit can work.

If we would but live the life of faith how wonderfully God would meet and bless us!

Galatians 5:25

Our next warning is found in the 25th verse of the fifth chapter. "If we live in the Spirit, let us walk in the Spirit."

Let me press upon you the great difference between the two things. Paul says you may have received the Holy Spirit when you believed, but that is not enough. You must also walk in the Spirit. It is possible for a man to separate the two things, one from the other. Men may be very anxious to get pardoned and become God's children, and yet think that after that they must be content to walk in the flesh. Look at pride, temper, worldliness, jealousy, coldness toward Christ, so little personal love. These are all the works of the flesh, and may be found in a man living in the Spirit and yet not walking in the Spirit. Now Paul comes to us and says that if we live in the Spirit we must also walk in the Spirit. What does that mean? Walk includes all our intercourse in daily life, our contact with people, our conversation with the world. All this must be in fellowship with the Spirit of God. Paul meant this Spirit to be in my home life, my church life, money making, money giving, money spending, every part of my life. Paul says that if you live in the Spirit, you should walk in the Spirit. Every step must be in the Spirit.

Am I preaching an impossible thing? Verily no. The message is the very mind of God and God's word. What did He send the Holy Spirit for, if it was not to enable His children to live a holy and a heavenly life? It was to sanctify us, to bring Christ into our lives and to make us one with Christ. In this chapter it is stated the fruit of the Spirit is love, joy, peace, long-suffering, gentleness,

goodness, faith, meekness, temperance.[123] How am I to live that?
Paul did not mean that for people who are better than we are. No,
it is for each of us. And how can I live thus? By being twice as
gentle or loving as I am? No! The fruit of the Spirit is love and
gentleness every moment of the day. But how am I to be kept every
hour of the day and walk thus in love? By having the filling of the
Spirit of God.

Are you going to take in this truth? I cannot live an hour of the day
rightly except as I am filled with the Spirit of God. Let us just give
up ourselves to walk in the Spirit and the power of the Holy Ghost
will become stronger and we will find there is grace to enable a
man to live and walk in the Spirit. This is a question of the deepest
importance. "Walk in the Spirit and ye shall not fulfill the lusts of
the flesh."[124] There is the answer to the question, how can I
conquer all these temptations of the flesh? Walk in the Spirit. Give
up to the Holy Spirit to rule your life, and you will not fulfill the
lusts of the flesh. You will not get out of the flesh, but you will have
power to conquer the flesh. The Holy Spirit will be the energizing
and dominating power in your life. That can be, because God has
promised it. If we yield our lives entirely with child-like faith, God
will lead us into that life.

Galatians 6:7-8

Last chapter, "Be not deceived, God is not mocked, for whatsoever
a man soweth that shall he also reap. For he that soweth to his
flesh shall of the flesh reap corruption; but he that soweth to the
Spirit shall of the Spirit reap life everlasting."[125]

The Galatians had gone back to the life of the flesh. They

---

[123] Galatians 5:22-23
[124] Galatians 5:16
[125] Galatians 6:7-8

worshipped God very earnestly but they were self-righteous. They thought to do a great deal to please God but all sorts of bitter jealousies and envyings broke out among them. Paul said they were in danger of devouring one another. When I do not wait for the Spirit of God to teach me and work in me then I cannot work in any other power than that of the flesh, and it brings me no real peace and happiness. Religious flesh, with its self-effort, is still sinful flesh. The man who is trying to conquer sin and serve God without the filling of the Holy Spirit finds sin stronger in Him every day, because he is trying to serve God in the power of the flesh. It is self, self-effort and self-confidence, and always breaks out into sin. There is no getting over this, we must not sow in the flesh, we must sow in the Spirit if we would reap the fruit of the Spirit. Our whole life is sowing. Every word we speak is sowing. Every action is a seed. Every sentiment and disposition is a seed. Let us sow in the Spirit. Let our whole life be a yielding to the Holy Spirit to perfect His life. We shall reap in the Spirit a great harvest of peace and power, of joy and blessing

Now, dear friends, there you have the warnings of the Epistle to the Galatians in regard to the holy life. I close by laying upon you the necessity of taking this truth to God in prayer, alone. My brother, the Father in heaven is waiting. As He looked upon the elder son, He looks upon us and says, "Thou art ever with Me and all I have is thine."[126] Why not come and claim what is ours? Let us go to the Father and implore Him to teach us the right life, the life of the Holy Spirit. Let us learn the lesson day by day, to be still and to yield ourselves to pray in the Spirit; to walk and work in the Spirit. Let us yield ourselves in faith to God, the Holy Trinity; the Father, through the Son gives the Holy Spirit to be the life of our soul. God make it your and my blessed experience every day.

---

[126] Luke 15:31

9. Be Filled with the Spirit
(second lecture)
(Ephesians 5:18)

I want to conclude these addresses on the Holy Spirit and His work in us, by a short summary of what that work is, showing the great and wonderful blessedness that the Holy Spirit brings to them that yield to Him. As my text I mean to take again the words that we have had before, Ephesians 5:18:

"Be filled with the Spirit."

I think we have said that we are in very great danger when we read that text of thinking of the Holy Spirit coming in great power, under a conscious sense of His presence, with a great stir of the emotions, with a great revelation of the glory of God, with a great quickening of our power for work; and yet very often this is not the case. I used the illustration of a river being filled up at once by heavy storms of rain, or a river being filled very gradually. I might speak again, of that same river.

Sometimes it is filled by the rain coming down in torrents, causing great noise and turmoil, and that same river might be filled with the water running down from the melted snow on the mountains, so that there will be a calm-like, steady rising, silently, without any noise or disturbance. And so the Holy Spirit may come with noise as of the sound of a rushing wind and with a wonderful thrilling throughout the whole being, yet many times He may come on the ordinary level of the daily life and a man can live filled with the Holy Spirit just while he is walking along quietly in his daily duties.

Then the great thing to know and understand is, what is it that the

Holy Spirit will work in such a man? I want to give you three very simple answers:

1. The Holy Spirit brings the presence of Christ
2. He gives the likeness of Christ
3. And the Holy Spirit works the power of Christ

1. The Holy Spirit is meant to give the presence of Christ.

You know, dear friends, that during the three years of Christ's work on earth, to the disciples, His presence was everything. Christ's presence met every trouble and supplied every need. When there were people around them the disciples knew that they had only to say to Christ, "Do help that woman," and it was done. There had been thousands around them without bread and they wanted to send them away, but Christ had only to tell them to bring five loaves and two fishes and the five thousand were fed.[127] The presence of Jesus was the supply of every need. They were in the storm and they cried, "Master, we perish."[128] The presence of Jesus in the ship was all that was needed. He said, "Peace, be still," and there was a great calm. When He appeared walking on the sea, they were terrified because they thought He was a spirit.[129] It was only necessary for Him to say, "Be not afraid," and their hearts were set at rest. When they wanted instruction, guidance or reproof, Christ's presence was their help. Everything depended upon having Christ with them. And now, in my life and yours, everything depends upon having Christ's presence with us. Christ's presence is very near and very clear and if I can get up in the morning, and if I can go through the day, and if I can meet every difficulty with the secret consciousness that the Lord Jesus, the Almighty One, is with me, then I am prepared for anything and my heart is kept in

---

[127] Matthew 14:13-21
[128] Matthew 8:23-27
[129] Matthew 14:22-33

perfect rest and in great joy.

But now, Christ was to go away to heaven and the hearts of the disciples were very sad, but listen, before He went away, He said, "I am coming again." "I will not leave you comfortless."[130] He told them that it was by the Holy Spirit He was coming to them. He promised them that He would pray the Father and that He would send the Comforter, He told them that if they loved Him, they would keep His commandments and then He promised to come and manifest Himself unto them, and that both He and the Father would come and take up their abode with them. Do you see that the Lord Jesus promised the Holy Spirit? He promised in the first place, above everything else, this: His abiding presence; and this is what the believer wants, and, dear friends, that is what our lives want. We don't know what it is to walk with Jesus as a little child walks with his father, and I want to press this upon you, the Lord Jesus is longing and willing to come so close to us and to stay so near to us that we can have His presence always.

This is not impossible—don't think it! Jesus is able to give us the consciousness of His abiding presence. And how does He do it? He does it by filling us with the Holy Spirit. This is the great work of the Holy Spirit: to glorify Christ. Remember the words John wrote when Christ said, "He that believeth on Me as the Scripture hath said, out of his belly shall flow rivers of living water. But this spake He of the Spirit which they that believe on Him should receive; for the Holy Ghost was not yet given; because that Christ was not yet glorified."[131] When Christ was glorified—when He had died and glorified the Father, and the Father had glorified Him in heaven— then the Holy Spirit came as the Spirit of Christ to show us Christ's heavenly glory, and that is why Christ says, "He shall glorify Me; He shall receive of mine, and shall shew it unto you."[132] The Holy

---

[130] John 14:18
[131] John 7:38-39
[132] John 16:14

Spirit is able to fill me with a real deep sense of the presence of Jesus Christ and of His glory. This is one of the essential roots of the Christian life: the presence of Jesus.

You have heard of what is called in England, the Keswick Movement. Keswick is in the north of England. The friends who are at the head of this movement stand for what they call the beginning of the spiritual life. Their great object is to show Christians how wrong and feeble their life is—sometimes light and sometimes dark, sometimes strong and sometimes weak—and to point out a better way. Many admit that they ought to live a different life. They are brought to the acknowledgment of what is wrong, to earnest self-searching, to give themselves up to God to be searched; and when the consciousness becomes strong and deep of what is wrong, then there is pointed out to them from God's word what the true life is. They don't talk so much about the baptism of the Holy Spirit at those conventions, but the most prominent thought is: Jesus Christ is the Savior from sin, and He is able to keep you always. They bring, by God's help, many to see that Jesus requires one step. This step only takes a moment. You don't have to wrestle, but just throw yourself in the arms of Christ and let that living Christ take hold of you, never letting Him go, but having Him with you all the day.

Out at the Cape I met a young missionary, just returned from Keswick, where he had been greatly blessed. I asked him what was the difference between his former life and now. He said it was just the personal friendship of Jesus. This is it: you know the Lord Jesus is such a dear friend, He is such a heavenly friend, and such a fountain of love—that is, if you get into the right relationship. Oh, then you must do it! The presence of Jesus must be like the sunlight, for the presence of Jesus makes everything bright. How can I get this, so that I have the Lord Jesus always with me, and I always know it, and I never get out of the realization of it for a minute? That is what Christ longs for. Don't think He is content with the way most Christians live. He is such a lover. He longs to be very near to us and have us wholly for Himself.

Listen friends, the way by which a man can always have the presence of Christ, is by the power of the Holy Spirit, and what is that way? Why, very simple. A man must confess, "I have not been living as I should, in close fellowship with Jesus. Sometimes I have met Him, but just as often I have forgotten and forsaken Him, living after my own heart, and although I have been kept from open sin, there has not been that holy warmth of a man whose walk is with his Lord. The Lord wants to have me always with Him, and the power of my Lord is to keep me always with Him, and the presence of my Lord is the only secret of a spiritual life." Believe this, say it, accept Him thus, in the fulness of His presence. Let me say that it is the wonderful purpose of God to make Jesus present with me every day and hour.

Dear friends, if your hearts long to know Jesus fully as the Deliverer from sin, as the comfort of your soul, are you willing to confess all of the sin of the past, bow down in shame, and be willing to be cleansed in the precious blood? Are you willing to give up yourself to a life of unbroken communion with Jesus? Oh, that God might work a deep desire in our hearts and make us all ready to say, "I want a life of unbroken communion with Jesus. I want Jesus to do the utmost He can for me. I want His love to rule and work through me all day. Is it possible?" The answer comes, "Have I not given the Holy Spirit, have I not sent the Holy Spirit into your heart for this one purpose, that He should always glorify Jesus in you?"

Oh come, believers, you have the Holy Spirit within you now, come and bow with shame and say, "Oh God, how little have I let the Holy Spirit manifest the presence of Jesus. Forgive me. Father, my heart responds and I want to open my whole being to Him; I want to yield entirely to Him; I want to be filled completely with the Holy Spirit that my whole being may be under His control, so that He may have power to reveal Christ always within me." If you will ask that, believe God's promises, claim its fulfillment, and say in deep humility and faith, "God is true, the Holy Spirit is here, the Holy Spirit can and will fill my heart, I am going to expect this, the presence of Jesus, kept in me, wrought in me, manifested in me by the Holy Ghost." God help us.

Dear friends, the first work of the Holy Spirit is to reveal the presence of Jesus.

2. The Holy Spirit gives the likeness of Christ

The Holy Spirit not only reveals the presence of Jesus, but He gives the likeness of Jesus. This is something additional. When a young Christian comes to understand what the presence of Jesus is, he finds how much there is of sin and flesh, self and failure, and shortcoming; and even though he has said he consecrated himself very humbly, and undividedly, he is very conscious of how much there still is that has not been consecrated and sacrificed, and the Holy Spirit will lead him on. The disciples had the presence of Jesus though they did not have His likeness. He was humble, they were proud, He was unselfish, they were selfish. Many want to have the presence of Jesus to keep them up, but they do not want to be entirely like Him. You cannot have that. They will say, "I cannot expect to be too holy. I want the presence of Jesus very near of course, but I don't expect to be very much like Jesus."

The Holy Spirit comes to reveal the presence of Jesus in you, not as a separate person, but as dwelling in your life and heart and disposition and character. The Holy Spirit wants to reveal the very likeness of Christ in you. The characteristics and disposition of Christ should all come to you. What are these characteristics, and what was His disposition? I cannot mention all, but it is a great thing, when looking on Christ's character, to find out what is His chief virtue? What is His chief characteristic? The answer is very simple: humility. Did He not say; "Take my yoke upon you and learn of Me, for I am meek and lowly in heart, and ye shall find rest to your souls."[133] Did He not continually speak about the Father, saying, "The Father hath sent Me."[134] He wanted people to know that He was a servant. He said, in substance, "I am not my own master, the words I speak are not mine, I don't speak of myself, I dare not speak one word of myself, but what I hear I speak. The works that I do I do not of myself, but the Father hath shown Me the works. I can do nothing of myself."[135]

Christ's life was a life of absolute dependence upon the Father, to do nothing of Himself, but just to let the Father teach Him, and let the Father work in Him, and let the Father carry out His will. "I seek not mine own honor, but the honor of Him that sent Me. There is another who honors my honor, I don't take care of that. I only take care of the honor of the Father. I came not to do mine own will, I have a will, but I gave it up, I came to do the will of the Father."[136] There was with Him a certain self-abnegation. He wanted to be nothing and God to be all. His chief virtue was humility. He gave God His place and glory; and what is the place and glory of God? That God should be all, and in all.

Christ came to man to take a humble place, to live as nothing. God told Him what to do. He tells the Father just to work in Him and show Him what to do. I am only to let God work out His purpose in me. That is the humility of Jesus. That is the Lamb of God. Some of you never thought of that. You have thought of His sacrifice for sin, and especially His blood, but you have never thought of His humility. Men must humble themselves and become nothing before God if they wish to return to Him. The Lord Jesus came from heaven and took that name—the Lamb of God—that He might prove to man He was the Lamb of God in littleness, meekness, gentleness and humility, and this is why Paul said, "He humbled

---

[133] Matthew 11:29
[134] e.g. John 5:36
[135] e.g. John 14:10
[136] See John 8:50,54

Himself, and became obedient unto death, even the death of the cross."[137] He virtually said, "Let it cost me what it will, I will do anything, I will die that God's will may be done."

Deep humility was the Spirit of Christ, and now when the Holy Spirit comes to us, does He come to bring us a very different disposition? You know the answer. The Holy Spirit wants to bring the likeness of Jesus in us—deep dependence upon God. This is what is wanted in the Church of Christ. There is so much pride, selfishness, unloving and self-seeking. May God help us to see the beauty of Christ, just to be in love with His humility and to believe that the Holy Spirit will breathe the humility of Christ into us.

Let me say something to you who are in earnest in seeking the filling of the Holy Spirit. I have spoken to more than one. Take a very earnest young man. He hears about this higher life. He says, "I want to get it;" he struggles, feels, and wills and cannot get it. Why? Because there is a great deal of self-will and self-trust in all that fighting. That is not the way to get it. How did Christ get the throne of glory? By going down into the grave, and God lifted Him up to the throne There is the place to get glory. You must sink down into death. It looks so difficult for you to understand what we mean. We tell you to be in earnest, we tell you to wrestle and make every sacrifice, we tell you to rest not till you get it, then fall down and become nothing—and yet both are true. A man must set his whole soul upon the price, and when he has struggled, he must begin to feel, "All my struggling cannot help me," and when that intense desire has been aroused, he must fall down with helplessness and say, "Lord, here I am. I can do nothing, I lie down, I die to self, I am in despair." When in utter despair the blessing comes.

Dear friends, the Holy Spirit is come to work out the likeness of Jesus in your hearts. Remember, as often as you read, "The likeness of Jesus," this is what the Holy Spirit is going to put into

---

[137] Philippians 2:8

my heart, whether it be self-sacrifice or whether it be humility, gentleness, or poverty before God.

Oh, do believe that the Holy Spirit is come to bring the likeness of Christ in you! When a soul has learned to look for this work with its blessings, say, "Lord, I want Thy presence; Lord, I want Thy likeness; Lord, I want Thy divine life; God help me to have my whole life filled with the Holy Spirit." God's answer: "Be filled with the Spirit."

3. The Holy Spirit works the power of Christ

The Holy Spirit brings us, not only the presence of Jesus and the likeness of Jesus, but third, the power of Jesus. We all speak about power for work and complain we have so little of it. Many of us are very earnest in prayer for the baptism of power; many of us cry for more power. All very good, but remember, "power belongeth unto God,"[138] and to Him alone. God has given the power to Christ, and Christ has said, "All power is given unto Me, in heaven and in earth,"[139] and there is not a shadow of spiritual power except in Christ—and Christ cannot give me power, as a thing to have in myself.

You all have been in some great manufacturing place or factory and seen the mighty engine which was the great fountain of power for moving all the machinery; not a spindle or wheel has any power of its own; it can only get power as it is in connection with the engine. Just so this Christ is a great fountain of power. He cannot communicate power to me if I have any secret power of my own, carrying about. If I want to be filled with the power of Jesus, as the machine must be in momentary connection with the steam engine, so my soul must be in momentary connection with Jesus; the

---

[138] Psalm 62:11
[139] Matthew 28:18

power is in Him, and He—the living Christ—wants to work through me. He said, "The Father worketh in me." Paul says, Colossians 1:29, "Striving according to His working, which worketh in me, mightily." I strive because God is working in me.

Dear friends, the church of Christ has a great work to do in the world. We have hardly touched the world. What machinery and what little result. We are accustomed to thinking of the work we have to do. Think of 800 millions of heathen who have never heard of Christ, and of the millions of nominal Christians who have nothing but the form of religion, without the power[140], and the tens of millions who are in the church, who may be God's own people, yet how worldly, how full of sin, and none can do this work but the living Christ.

He can do it, and will do it, but how? If the Holy Spirit reveals Christ within me, my heart will be strengthened and I will learn to love souls more and care for them, and speak to them in the power of Christ. Do not think that is impossible. When a man speaks in the power of Christ there will be fruit. How can I have this power of Christ working in me? How can I preach a sermon tomorrow, visit some unconverted man? Or, how can I always allow the power of Christ to work through me? Listen, I must be filled with the Spirit of God, then Christ can work with me.

You long for power for service. Jesus Christ is the wisdom and the power of God. Get linked to Him by faith that sees and knows from moment to moment. His power will work in you. As the leather band brings power from the great steam engine from moment to moment, the Holy Spirit will keep your heart waiting and trusting in the presence and power of Christ which will be revealed, and it will not be you that works but Christ working in you. "Be filled with the Spirit."

---

[140] 2 Timothy 3:5

As I said some days ago, we take up, next week, studies on 'The person of Jesus Christ,' and this is our concluding address in regard to the work of the Holy Spirit. Shall we gather up, in one or two thoughts, all? Dear friends, let us bow very low and very humbly in the thought, that the Great Spirit of God is waiting to get complete possession. Oh, the mystery! Oh, the blessing! The Great Spirit of God is waiting to get full possession and I cannot force Him, I cannot grasp Him, but I can lie down at the foot of my God and say, "Father, fill me with Thy Spirit."

Oh, give up yourself in emptiness, in surrender, as Jesus gave Himself unto death and the grave, and remember that God raised Him to the throne of glory and gave Him the Holy Spirit to give to us. Sink down into your nothingness and helplessness in the grave of Jesus and God will lift you up and fill you with the Holy Spirit. Often He has done it. Let us then cultivate an intense longing after righteousness. Let us fall down very low and humble ourselves before God. Never mind if there are difficult questions, there is God's promise, God's gift and God's power. Wait upon God and He will give you the filling of the Holy Ghost.

Lastly, believe! believe! believe! with a desperate faith. "I am convinced God means me to be filled with the Holy Spirit." Say it. Trust God for it. Trust God for it. Sink low down, first, with your whole heart, and look to God and He will fill you. May it be the blessed experience of everyone. Let us bow in prayer.

10. Christ Bringing us to God
(1 Peter 3:18)

The words I wish to speak on you, find in 1 Peter 3: 18:

"Christ, also, hath suffered for sins, the just for the unjust, that He might bring us to God."

They went into the great object of Christ's work. What was it for that He came? "That He might bring us to God."

You know there is a great difference in a way to a house and the house itself. I may be traveling through the most beautiful scenery, on a lovely, pleasant day, with delightful company, and enjoying every step of the way, and yet I am not content to stay there always. I have gone into that way to bring me to the end, the object of my journey. Christ is the way; what is the end of the way? The end is God. Christ wants to bring us to God.

You often find Christians so occupied with Christ that they never get time for God. You ask me, is there any difference between going to Christ and going to God? A very great difference. In Christ I have the gracious and merciful side of God's character. But that is not the only side of the divine character I need to know. In Christ I have the condescension of God coming near to me, but the object of that condescension is to bring me back to righteousness and holiness. You can never have true strength and an all-round Christian experience unless you learn the lesson that Christ is going to win your heart that He may bring you back to God.

Just think, Christ was not in Himself self-sufficient when He was on earth. He lived every day with the thought within Him: "There is one greater than I[141], and my blessedness is to live in dependence upon Him, with a will given up to His will and in a trust that counts upon His working." And if I am to be in Christ and Christ in me, what was His life must become my life: fellowship with God and dependence upon God.

There are aspects of the divine character that are more fully revealed in God the Father than in God the Son. Take, for instance, the fear of God. I never, in the New Testament, read of the fear of Christ. He came to reveal the other side, the love and the attractiveness and the trust worthiness of God. The element of fear and holy reverence was an element in Christ's own character. Do not I read in Hebrews, the fifth chapter, that when Christ prayed He was heard in that He feared.[142] He had godly fear towards the Father, and if my Christian character is to be perfect and all-around, I must have the fear of God as it is revealed in the Old Testament working into the very foundations of my life; with this most child-like confidence there must ever be a deep, deep fear of God before the throne.

I read that the four living creatures and twenty-four elders cast their crowns before the throne.[143] I read that angels and seraphim veil their faces with their wings.[144] If my Christian character is to be perfect there must be in it that deep consciousness of the inconceivable greatness of God above me that makes me bow in the very dust before Him. And it is just because so many Christians have never given the truth a right place in their hearts that Christ came to bring them to God—that there is so wanting in them that blessed element of fear and reverence, worship and adoration.

---

[141] John 14:28
[142] Hebrews 5:7
[143] Revelation 4:4
[144] Isaiah 6:2

Come, let us think what this means. Christ came to bring us to God. I am not going to try and give you a theological essay upon the atonement. You know all about that. But I want to look at the practical side. My object is to help the beloved workers who are being trained in this Institute, not so much as to right comprehension and clear thought, but to the down-right practical life, such as God would have. If we could get a step nearer that life all our study and work will be brighter and more entirely in the power of the Holy Spirit.

How can I make it clear that Christ brings men to God? I think I can answer it in this way: we need, in our practical, everyday life, to be brought nigh to God and to be living in that nearness. Let me take the morning hour of prayer. A man wakes up in the morning with the thought, "Christ is come to bring me nearer to God. How am I to begin the day if I am to live near to God?" That is what the heart longs for. Well, come, just let us think how Christ brings us near to God. A man's desire to walk before God is strong. He wants to be as full of God as he can be. How is he to attain it? I want to give a few practical thoughts.

1. I think, first of all, he must set himself to give God the place that belongs to Him.

If I want to be brought nigh to a person, I want to know who that person is. If he is a king or emperor, I approach him with a different feeling from what I approach a slave. If I approach a friend, thoughts of joy fill me. Before I am brought to God, I must know who God is; and as I bow before Him, I must say, "He is the Almighty One, the All Holy One. He cannot bear sin or the shadow of sin. He wants to take it away. He is the All Loving One, He wants to communicate Himself to me. The Everywhere Present One, who is with me and able to make Himself known to my soul." If I want to be brought nigh to God I must first say, "He is God, and my soul must bow in lowly stillness and in an attitude of faith, and just exercise the belief: God is here. He—the Creator of all things on the earth, the Incomprehensible One; He is a consuming fire; He is love and wants to impart Himself wholly to me. *That* God is near. But I do not know Him; I know so little of Him, how can I come nigh to Him?"

2. Then next I begin to think, "Who am I?" and I say, "If I give God His place, I must take the right place for myself."

I am a creature and I have nothing holy. I have nothing good except what God gives me. I am nothing except a vessel in which God can show forth His glory, and therefore I want to take my place before God as nothing. If Christ is to bring me to God, I must sink down into my nothingness. I am not only a creature, but I am a sinner. That ought to make me take a still lower place. Paul never could forget that He was the chief of sinners.[145] He was always thinking of that time before his conversion when he persecuted Christ and the disciples, so he bowed low in his old age and said, "I am the chief of sinners." He was not talking about his daily sins. He was talking about the more than twenty years before, when he was a blasphemer. You know, if you are to meet the Emperor of China there are certain rules about bowing before him. And there are certain rules if I am to meet God. I must come in deep self-abnegation. And then I am a redeemed sinner; this humbles me still more. I take the lowest place. There is God waiting for me to hear my cry. How can I have intercourse with this God? Jesus Christ brings me to God.

3. Take the third step. The first was: give God His place and let Him be seated on His throne of glory; the second: take your place before God. The third: take your place in Christ Jesus.

---

[145] 1 Timothy 1:15

I am speaking to believers. You understand what the atonement is—that we have been brought nigh by the blood. You have believed that for yourself personally—that your sins are pardoned and you have had access to God's favor. You want, this morning, to be brought into a life always near to God. You need Christ to do it! How can He do it? Take your place in Christ Jesus and by an act of faith and by the light of the Holy Spirit, see and believe that you are one with Christ. Christ is before the Father and you are in Him and He is in you. No branch was ever so really in the vine, no finger of my hand was ever so truly in my body, as I am in Christ by a vital union, and as Christ is in me. And when I want to come to God, I am told that the place I am to occupy is the place of the most intimate nearness.

The writer of the Hebrews teaches it. The efficacy of the blood is our boldness; the living High Priest waits to bring us in.[146] It is not that I am down here while He does a little work in and for me. No! As the High Priest who says, "Ye in Me, and I in you," He brings me to God. In the power of my union with Him, in living fellowship with Himself, He presents me; and I by faith have a real, abiding access within the veil—into the very life, into the very heart and love of God. There I bow in holy adoration and speak the words,

> "So near, so very near to God
> More near I cannot be
> For in the person of His Son
> I am as near as He."[147]

Christ came to bring us unto God. I am not only in Him, but Christ is in me as a living person. Christ takes charge of me. Christ introduces me to the Father, and as I am before the Father, Christ gives the working of the Holy Spirit and He teaches me what my work is when I am brought nigh to God. It was that God might get

---

[146] Hebrews 4:14-16
[147] *A Mind At Perfect Peace With God* by Horatius Bonar

His children in a life of fellowship to understand and realize who He is.

Some, when they get within the veil, when they are brought nigh into the holiest of all, look upon it as a grand attainment. It is only the beginning of the blessed life. For when I am there, then God is able to let His light shine into my whole being. Then God is able to let His holiness come upon me. When I am there, God is able to make me bow and sink down into a nothingness and into humility that I never thought possible to attain to—that I may be there receiving the inflowing of God's Holy Spirit in a freshness and a fullness inconceivable.

Oh, beloved, Christ came to bring us very nigh to God! It is not only nearness of acceptance but nearness of love—the consciousness that He loves me and I love Him. It is the nearness of that union of love which consists in the closest possible fellowship. Give up all in emptiness for Him to fill, and God waits to come down and pour His fullness into me. Christ died that He might bring us unto God, and in that place—in God's presence—oh, there it is that not only God's work in me is to be done, but there it is I am to learn how to do my work for God. In that nearness to God is the place of intercession.

Throughout the church of Christ there is a universal complaint that we pray too little. Some work much but pray little. We pay far more attention to what we have to do with men than to what we have to do with God. Beloved, the fountains of the Christian life, the fountains of the outflow of the Holy Ghost, the fountains of love and power to be broken up in our hearts and to be poured out to men—these fountains rise from the throne of God, and it is only as man tarries before God in fellowship with the Most High, that God's love can flow through us.

Ask any worker of experience, ask any man who has preached the gospel long, and he tells you he has to mourn the fact that he has not had that deep love for sinners which comes from dwelling in the love of God. And where am I to receive this inflowing love? It is when I am brought nigh to God. There it is I learn what intercession is; there I become strong to bear the burden of the church and of the world in quiet pleading with God. I have such access to Him, I am so really His friend, He gives me such power with Him, that I know I have only to plead and an answer will come.

Dear friends, is there not a great deal of our living of which we might confess it bears but little mark of Christ having brought us nigh to God?

4. There is another step. I say Christ brings us thus nigh to God in Himself that we may act out and live our lives in the world in that nearness to God.

You occasionally find men, when they speak in public, they have a sense of God upon them. I have been told that at the great International Convention in London, there was more than one speaker of great eloquence, but there was one man whose very presence, when he rose to speak, hushed the audience. The very presence of God was with him. So, with a man like George Müller, who has spent his whole life in prayer—the presence of God is on him. But how seldom one finds this! Of George Bowen of India, it is told that he had said that the nearness of God was nearer unto him than any man upon earth. A friend asked him about it, and his answer was: "Yes, God is nearer to me, consciously, than anyone in this room." Is it not that presence we want? That presence of God to go out and meet men, to go out and do work, to go out and engage in business, to go out and be tempted and tried, the presence of the Everlasting God to be with us from morning to night, moment by moment.

You ask me, "Can it be?" I ask you—I have asked it before, I ask it again—does it cost you any trouble to enjoy the sunlight from moment to moment, whether you pick up a book to read or whether you look into the face of a friend to recognize him, or whether you do business or domestic work? The sun takes care to shine all along. God has given it to you. It does its work. You spend every moment of the day in the enjoyment of that light. And what think you? Would your God care more to have such provision made for your body than for your spirit? We need not be in the dark without the light of the sun twelve hours of the day, and would God not be able and make provision that you should every moment abide in the light of His presence and the joy of His immediate nearness?

Christ came and died to bring us unto God. Listen to what we read in the Hebrews, about the better hope of the New Testament "by which we draw nigh unto God."[148] Listen to what we read in the same chapter, "He is able to save completely them that come to God by Him."[149] If you will learn not only to ask this blessing among other blessings, but if you will indeed believe that Christ will fulfill this work in you and bring you nigh unto God so that every moment of your life is spent in His presence, Christ will work it out in your life. Christ suffered that "He might bring us to God."

Dear friends, as surely as we are God's children, our life can be full of God. In Ephesians, Paul tells us that God is willing to strengthen us with might by His Spirit in the inner man[150], until we are filled with the fullness of God or unto the fullness of God[151]. I long thought that meant some high experience, but it means simply that God wants to be present with us with such consciousness that our heart is all the time full of His blessed presence, His holy will and His divine inworking. Christ wants to bring us nigh to God!

---

[148] Hebrews 7:19
[149] Hebrews 7:25
[150] Ephesians 3:16
[151] Ephesians 3:19

One more thought. When Christ brings us nigh to God, He brings our will in perfect harmony to the will of God. I cannot have my will at variance with God's will, or mourning its inability to do God's will, and all the time have the enjoyment of the blessing of God's light and God's presence.

Christ came to bring me to God. I not only need faith to realize that He is in me and I in Him, but by faith I need to give myself up to His working—that as a living person He shall reveal the will of God perfectly in me, and so breathe into me His own disposition and His own life. Christ is to dwell and live in me. I am not to count Christ as a separate being, dwelling in my heart as a locality, but Christ is to be in my heart, in my life, in my thinking, living and willing, as the very life of all I do, so that He lives Himself out through me. So, Christ is formed in me and God sees the very figure, the very form of Christ within me. And as Christ is thus manifested within me in His disposition and Spirit, the nearness of God becomes more intimate and the fellowship with God becomes more close.

Oh, beloved, God wants us to come nigh to Him in Christ! Are there not many Christians who live far from God? When you press this thought, they are satisfied with having been pardoned and brought nigh. You have reason to doubt your position unless you have yielded to God to work out the practical, spiritual, experimental nearness to God. We talked, last week, about the baptism of the Holy Spirit, and the baptism of power, and the life of the Spirit, but I do pray you—young men and women, who are going to devote yourselves to service, and you believers who are longing to live holy lives—remember one thing: you want more of God in your life.

A man has just as much religion as he has of God, and if a man wants more religion, he must have more of God. We have a great deal of seeking of more religion, more power, and yet we do not think of having more of God. God created you for Himself to fill you with Himself. Christ redeemed you to be filled with your God. Oh, come and let Christ do His work, and before we go on to speak this evening about that life, let us realize this one supreme thought: Christ wants to bring me to God.

I want, by the help of God, to be very practical, and I want to ask believers, is this what you are seeking for? Have you come here for the acquiring of new truths or thoughts, or are you here that Jesus may bring you near to God? When you pray, two minutes spent in quietly giving yourself to be brought near to God by Christ would be better than twenty minutes in prayer in the ordinary way. We often pour out our petitions, praise and confessions to a distant God. If you want your life changed, if you want God to come into your life, if you want God to take possession of your life, in prayer always make your first desire: "Son of the Father, bring me near to God." Bow in the very deepest adoration and reverence and wait, wait before Him.

It is God's own work to reveal Himself. Bow in an act of faith: "The Everlasting God is here, longing to take possession of me, willing to make Himself known. I wait upon God." Bow in deep lowliness, and beseech God, for His great mercy's sake, to come near and make Himself known to you. I often see young Christians, how they try to grasp every truth and rejoice over every beautiful conception. They resolve to live entirely for God and they know not how much self-confidence there is in all. I pray that God may bring them to the place of feebleness and emptiness.

You know Peter's consecration. It was such a defective consecration. He said, "I am ready to go to prison and death." He truly meant it, but it was in self-confidence. Christ led him to see it when He allowed him to fall. Then he was humbled and wept bitterly. I beseech you, pray to God with your whole heart, "Oh God, make me humble, make me meek, make me gentle, and let the glory of God fill my soul with fear and reverence all the day!" Do not be afraid that it will take away your joy. It will strike deeper root into the very depth of your being.

Christ suffered, that He might bring us to God. What did He suffer? Nothing was too great. He endured all that He might bring us to God. Are you willing to take time and trouble that you may be brought nigh to God? If that has become the object of our desires, we will understand the work of Christ far better, and our understanding and knowledge of that work will bring far more abundant fruit.

11. Christ Liveth in Me
(John 15:1–12)

I want to speak, this evening, about the life that Christ lives in us. You have it here in the Parable of the Vine.[152] What can be closer or more intimate than the union between the vine and the branch? How the very same sap that is in the vine is to be found in the branch. We have very many kinds of grapes, but in each case the juice that is in the vine is the very same juice that is in the branch. And so the very same life and Spirit which is in Christ is to be in us. This is the great lesson we want to learn tonight. Read John 15:1–12. Our life is to be a life of perfect union with Jesus. Let us join in prayer and ask God to reveal to us something of the wonderful glory of the life that we have in Christ Jesus, and let us believe that He can, even now, give us definite blessing.

We want to have a clear idea of what we, in our Christian life, aim at. The question is: what is the work that Christ does to bring us nigh to God? In what way does He enable us to live as God wants us to live? I said this morning that we too often think of Christ as an outward person here on earth who hears and helps us. A man may come and give me $10,000 and so be my helper, but there is no further union between him and me. The man may be a great benefactor, but there is no organic union between him and me. I may never see him again. Many people look upon Christ as such a separate, outward Savior. They never can fully enjoy His salvation. I must believe that even as Christ is in heaven, so He is here in me, His branch. He comes into my inmost life, He occupies that life, He lives there, and by living there He enables me to live as a child of God.

---

[152] John 15:1-12

Some think that when Christ dwells within us He comes somewhere in the region of the heart and He lives there. We are two separate persons—Christ one and I one—and somehow He works in me at times. No! That is not the way. Christ comes into me and becomes my very life. He comes into the very root of my heart and being. He comes into my willing and thinking and feeling and living, and lives in me in the power which the Omnipresent God alone can exercise. When I understand this, my soul bows down in adoration and confidence toward God. I live in the flesh— the life of flesh and blood—but Christ dwelling in me is the true life of my life. The words which I want to speak are very simple and well-known. Galatians 2:20: "Christ liveth in me. I am crucified with Christ, nevertheless I live, yet not I, but Christ liveth in me."

Now, the point to which I want to direct attention this evening is that if Christ is to live in me, He does not live in me by a blind force, nor without my knowing it. He calls me to come and see what His life is, and so if I desire His life, I must give up mine. I must also give up all wrong ideas about what the life of Christ really is. I cannot have the life of Christ in power in me unless I seek to know truly what the life is that He lived.

Oh, come and let the living Christ live in you! And to that end, seek to know the life He has set before you in His example. Not that we are able to imitate Christ. But because Christ lived His life for us and imparts it to us, therefore we can do it. What folly it would be for a child of three years to say, "All that my father can do I can do." And how can I say, "I can live as the mighty Christ did"? What folly to attempt to walk as Christ did! And yet, the Bible tells me I must do it. The Bible also tells me I can do it, because "Christ liveth in me."[153] If I allow the living Christ to take possession of my will and desires, I can walk even as He walked.

Let us come to the life of Christ and try and find out what is that

153 Galatians 2:20

life that He lived on earth with His Father. That is exactly the Christ who liveth in us. There are not two Christs, only one. The Christ that lived on earth is the Christ that lives in my heart. The great mark of Christ is that He lived in the deepest humility and dependence upon the Father. He said, "I can do nothing of Myself."[154] In everything He had His life from God.

Note five points in His life:

1. Take His birth. There He received His life from God.

2. Take His life and walk on earth. He always waited upon God. He lived His whole life in dependence upon God alone.

3. Take His death. He gave up His life to God, even unto the very death.

4. Take His resurrection. He received His life back again from God the second time.

5. Take His ascension. He was taken up to heaven to find His glory with God.

Don't you see? From the beginning to the end, God was everything in that life. If I understand that—that the Christ who is going to live in me is the Christ that honored God in everything—He will work that same disposition in me. And that will be the beauty, blessedness and strength of my life, when I learn like Christ to know that in everything God is all, and when the motto of His life becomes mine: "For God, to God, through God, are all things."[155]

1. His birth

Look at the birth of Christ. What does that mean? God gave the power of the Holy Spirit in the Virgin Mary, and it was by the

---

[154] John 5:30
[155] Referencing Romans 11:36

almighty power of God that Christ was born as a child in Bethlehem. He was the workmanship of God. God sent the Holy Spirit to form Him and to work everything in connection with His birth in the Virgin Mary. Christ always remembered that. He always told the people His Father sent Him. He was not His own master. He acknowledged that He had been sent by God. He always acknowledged that He had His life from God. The Father hath given all things into the hands of the Son. "The Father hath given unto the Son to have life in Himself."[156] That was Christ's starting point. "My life comes from God. I come from God. I have nothing of myself, and everything I get I must get from God."

Now, if Christ took that stand, I wish that we could be brought to take that stand and to say in deep truth, "This new life is a life that I have from God. God gave it me. I have got a work of God right in my heart, by the Holy Ghost, in regeneration. I have got a new life from God." And what will you then think of that life that God has given? Who is going to maintain it? God alone can maintain what He has begun. He must work it out to completion. He must perfect it to the very end. So, my life is given by God. The life of Christ and the life of my soul are both given from God in heaven, received from Him, and must be kept day by day in deep consciousness, it belongs to God.

2. His life

God alone can keep it right, maintain it. It is the highest folly for me to think I can keep it myself. Have you ever studied that? I have received from the living God, the living Christ in me; and I am not to try and live out that life, but I am to take it to God and acknowledge, "My God, Thou hast planted it in me; Thou, alone, canst keep it." Do this if you want to realize what that dependence is—how Christ lived His whole life in dependence upon God's will

---

[156] John 5:26

and God's strength and God's might. He said, regarding that question of strength, "The Son can do nothing of Himself."[157] Was that really true? Yes. He said, "The words I speak, I speak not of Myself, but as the Father showeth the works, them I do."[158] He said in regard to His will, "I came not to do my own will."[159] "I cannot trust my will. I do not know what I ought to do. I wait fully, that the Everlasting God might work out what is right."

If Christ, the Holy One, needed to say that, don't you think you and I need it ten thousand times more? And that is what we want Christ to come into us for: to breathe in us that very disposition, and that is what I speak of. The very highest virtue of any Christian life is only to let God have His way. Only to give God the opportunity of doing His work in us, and coming day by day, hour by hour, to the place of absolute dependence upon God; and to learn one lesson: "Oh God, I have nothing! I do not know anything, I am nothing—nothing—and I can only do what God makes me."

And now, how is Christ to bring me near to God? He cannot bring me near to God in any other way than the way He came Himself. What was that way? The way of the deepest self-abnegation—the way of the most entire surrender to God. He was forever expecting God to work in Him, to look to God for strength. He prayed to God for guidance. He cried to God in His trouble. God was everything—everything—to Him, and Christ was content to be nothing. Are you willing to have this Christ to come into your life?

Dear friends, I cannot speak it out plain enough in words. The great reason why our Christian life does not advance more is: we try to do too much ourselves. We are far too self-active and self-confident. We, perhaps, never learned the simple elementary lesson that the only place for me before God is just to be nothing

---

[157] John 5:19
[158] John 14:10
[159] John 6:38

and God will work in me.

Look at the angels in heaven, the seraphim and cherubim. Why are they such bright flames before the throne of God? Because they are nothing. Nothing in them to hinder God, and He can let the glory of His presence burn right through them. And why was Christ so perfect, and why did Christ gain such victory, and why did Christ please God so? It is this one reason: He allowed God to work in Him from morning until night, and every step was just in dependence upon God. He said, "Father, guide me," "Father, I wait upon Thee," "Father, work in me." And when Christ comes to live in us, do believe me and God's word, the first and chief thing He wants to work in you is an absolute dependence upon your God.

Christians, have you not to confess, "I have never seen that right. I have not lived it out. I have not understood that from morning to night I must let God work in me. I must do nothing"? You may say, "How can we do our work? Was Christ also inactive? Was the Apostle inactive?" With a restless activity he traversed the world, and yet all the time he says, "I am nothing." Waiting upon God won't make us inactive. It will give us a higher activity. Pray to God to teach us that Christ in us needs a life of absolute, entire dependence upon God.

3. His death

Look at the death of Christ. What does that mean? It means that the life that God had given, He gave that up entirely to God; and that means this: He said, "I have no wish to regard my life as my own property. If God wants it—however much suffering, however much shame and death it costs me—if God wants it, I give it up to God." That is fair. That is right. If I have everything from God then everything ought to return to God. Thus with Christ. That had been His whole life through, for His death was nothing but the completion of the spirit that had indicated all His life. When He was only twelve years old, remember, He said to Mary, "Know ye not I must be about my Father's business?"[160] And time after time He said, "It is my meat and drink to do the will of Him that sent me."[161] "I am not come to do my own will, but the will of Him that sent Me."[162] And so He went down to Gethsemane, where He said to the Father, "Not my will but Thine be done."[163]

I am afraid we have never acknowledged the right that God has, and that we have never understood: every power I have comes straight from God, my whole life comes from God, and every moment of my life ought to go back to God, and every strength I get in the spiritual life comes from God just as the sunlight comes from the sun, and everything ought to go back to God, and every action will be to the glory of God.

A Christian who has Christ in him will be a man truly sacred and given up wholly to God. Is that easy? No. Why? Because self is in us so strong. The curse of sin has brought us into that fearful condition, that instead of considering it an honor and a privilege to be nothing and to do His will, we have come to look upon it as hard. We have come to look upon it as a high attainment, indicating that we cannot attain to it. If a man gives up himself, and will come to God, he can live this life of Christ living in him, or else the Bible cannot be true.

Paul, writing in the Epistle to the Colossians, prayed for the Colossians, that they might "stand perfect and complete in all the will of God." Colossians 4:12. Beloved, listen! Christ only lived for God's will—and do you want that Christ in your hearts, or do you want to try and live a little for your own will? Do you want the living Christ, the Christ that reveals God, the living Christ who gave up everything—do you want that Christ? Oh, come now, if there is

---

[160] Luke 2:49
[161] John 4:34
[162] John 6:38
[163] Luke 22:42

any man who has a right to say it, it is Christ! This is what I want—
such a Christ to live in me. A Christ that will enable me to live in
dependence upon God, and in surrender to God. God gives you this
Christ if from the heart you give up your life, time and will to God
to do that very special thing in me.

What does it mean? It means a great deal. There was that beautiful,
perfect life of Christ, without one sin. Was it necessary to give up
that life? Yes. Because that life of Christ was connected with us,
and Adam, who were in the power of sin; and God said if He
wanted a life of everlasting glory, the life with us connected with
Adam and sin must be laid down in death. Christ said, "What shall
I do? I want to be glorified with the Father." He had prayed,
"Father, glorify Thy Son."[164] He felt, "I cannot have the two lives. I
cannot take this life that I got from the flesh, that is in the likeness
of the flesh, to heaven. It cannot be." So, the question came, "Will
you give up this life that you have from Adam, under the curse of
sin? Will you give it up if God will give you a life of everlasting
glory?" Christ said, "Yes."

Christ says, "If you want Me to live in you, you must do what I did.
Your own life must be given up to the very death, unto the death of
the cross, to be crucified." I must die to self, I must die to the
world, I must be an actual partaker of the death of Christ. "If we
are planted in the likeness of His death, we shall be raised in the
likeness of His resurrection."[165] I must say to God, "I must seek to
lose my life, and I want to die to self, and I want Him to come into
me with His death, and to take me down into it.

4. His resurrection

Fourth step: Resurrection. What does that mean? It means that

---

[164] John 17:1
[165] Romans 6:5

when Christ laid down His life into the grave, that God gave it back to Him in double glory. When Christ had gone down into the grave and into death, God lifted Him up and gave Him a new life infinitely higher and better than the life He laid down. That teaches me this: that if I am willing to lay down my evil life, my evil will, my heart and its affections, all my power in this world, to give it all up to God, to die to it, and to give up myself wholly to trust and wait upon God, God will give the new and resurrection life of Christ, in my heart, here on earth. Christ the Living One who was raised from death will come and live in my heart. "As He was dead, and is alive, for evermore."[166]

Study the grave of Jesus. What does it mean? Christ gave Himself up unto death—utter helplessness—to be nothing before God; and there He lay, just allowing God to take His time to do His work. When He was in the grave, in darkness, in death, He left it to God to do what might please Him. What did God do? God fulfilled His promise and gave Him a life a thousand times more glorious than that life sacrificed on Calvary. Listen, if you want Christ to really live in your heart, you want that Christ who went down into the grave. He had trusted God and was raised by God again. You want Christ with the resurrected life to come into you and be one with you, the Christ who was dead and is alive for evermore, and comes and brings the power of His death in me, so that everything dies to self and sin and brings the power of His life, so that everything in me can live with a new life from God—even Jesus Christ that wants to live in me.

I do beseech you, do not let yourselves be deceived with some thoughts about the presence of Jesus. Just think of Him specially in me. Trust in Him. Let it become a reality. Let Him become a live presence. Who is this Christ who lives in me? He is a man who received His life from God, who lived that life in intimate dependence upon God, a man who gave up His whole life and will

---

[166] See Revelation 1:18

to God, the man raised from the dead by the almighty power of God. This is the Christ to live in you.

5. His ascension

Last. After His resurrection, He ascended up into heaven. It means that God took Him up into the place of power, to share with Him in His throne of glory, to make Him partaker of that divine power by which the Holy Spirit is to become a blessing to the world. There are some who cry, "How can I be a blessing to my fellow men?" How did Christ become a blessing to the world? He gave Himself up to God, and He died to Himself and to His own natural life and waited for God to raise Him up. And because He did so, God lifted Him up to the place of blessing. He gave Him the fullness of the Holy Spirit to give you. You want Christ. He is in heaven. But oh, my brother, you cannot have Christ until you have learned the lesson of depending upon God, to die, and then you must learn by faith to claim Christ in the resurrection and in the ascension—and thus as Jesus Christ lives in you in your earthly life you will become a sharer of the glory of His heavenly love. The whole Christ-life in you—the Christ-dependence upon God, the Christ given up to God, the Christ raised up by God, and the Christ exalted above with God—this Christ wants to come and live in you!

If Christ is to bring me near to God then it cannot be as an outward person. He up in heaven and He dwelling and living in me. How is Christ going to bring me near to God? Only one way: Christ must live in my heart. He must live in me by united harmony and oneness of faith towards that God. This is a spiritual mystery, but God is a Holy Spiritual Being, and I cannot draw nigh to Him by my thought nor by thinking about a certain locality of heaven. Being brought to God means that Christ comes into me and lives His life in me and leads me up into personal fellowship with the Living God.

Now the great question that stirs the church is: why are Christians

so feeble? And the great question with many is: what can we do to
get the full Christian life, to live as God promises we can live? What
can we do to become just such children of God as the Father is able
to make us—branches of the Living Vine, to the glory of God? My
beloved Christians, let me bring you to the point. What have you to
do? First of all, we must look upon this Christ and ask ourselves,
"Am I willing to give up everything, that this Christ can live in me?"
You saw and know how Christ lived in Paul. Why, it was as if Christ
had become incarnated in Paul! The same zeal for God, same love
for souls, and same readiness to sacrifice everything. Everything
great in Paul was the complete Christ-life in him. There have been
Christians since that day that you could see the very form of Christ
in them.

Now, are you willing to have such a Christ? Suppose this were
possible, if God were to offer any one of us that were willing for it.
Suppose you were to be as poor as Christ was, as persecuted as He
was, and suppose God were to say, "My children, I am giving the
highest glory to man, to allow the Christ to come and live in him
and live this suffering life that He lived." How many of us would
say, "Yes, Lord, I would give anything that Christ might take
possession of me"? How many would say, "Here in Chicago, I
cannot do it. It would cost too much in business to take Him in me
that way." Oh friends, God comes to us with that question! "Are
you willing to have my Son, Jesus, as you find Him in the Word—in
His humility, in His dependence, in His submission and obedience,
in His surrender to death and the grave, in His waiting upon God
to raise Him—are you willing to have that Christ live in your
heart?"

Some men want life to study. They never get enough wisdom. They
long for knowledge. Are there none willing, tonight, to ask God to
make them willing. I feel that it is time to be trusting Jesus. My life
is so unlike Jesus, and yet He gave His blood for it. Are there not
here some who are willing to say, "Lord God, help me, I do desire
to have this life and this Christ in me." Is there someone trembling,

perhaps?

I had a note from someone this morning. They said they were afraid they were not willing to take the step God requires. They said, would I pray that they might be willing. Well, I do not know whether the writer is here, but I know that there is someone that feels, "I am afraid I am not willing to let the real Christ, just as He lived on earth, live in me. I am not ready to live a life of real dependence upon God, every minute in the presence of God. I am not willing to give up all my pleasure and will."

Are you willing? It looks hard, but are you willing to come? If you cannot say that are you willing to, say that you are willing to be made willing to come. I say, "Do you will to be made willing? Very well, do it." Say, "We can come." I would to God that everyone here were willing. Oh come, though your heart is so feeble! Say, "I do want that Christ to live, completely, His own life in me, and just reproduce His own life and make me exactly like Himself, to live for man, in Him." He is ready.

Beloved, you have often and often heard the gospel—and heard the gospel of sanctification and consecration and obedience—but have you understood, and have you accepted this truth, that it just means letting go everything, and letting Christ have all? Are you willing? Are you willing to pray, "God make me willing, tonight? Your life can be changed, and then comes the second question. If you are willing, are you going in fully to trust God tonight—to take you and to begin this great work in you by letting the life of Christ have perfect dominion? Are you willing to say, "I want to become all Christ can make me? I want to please God in everything. I do want Christ to do His best in me. I want to give myself to Christ, to let Him have everything." Will you not tonight believe an Everlasting Almighty Christ is waiting and willing, ready and able to take possession of you? Yes! Shall I not tonight claim Christ as my indwelling Lord and say, "Son of God, why wilt Thou not take me wholly for Thyself? It looks hard, and dark, and impossible, but

I am going to trust Thee, Thou Lamb of God. I long to be brought into the very closest union."

Oh man and woman, you are Christians! Do not be contented any longer with a half-hearted Christianity. Saying, "I am saved, and pardoned. I have got a little of Christ, I do my best." Oh, come to the full life that God offers you! Let Christ take entire possession. Let Christ come in. The Humble One, the Obedient One, the Suffering One, the Dying One, the One who lived in dependence upon God, and say, "That shall be my life if Christ will live in me. Oh God, Lord, I am willing, and I know Thou art willing. I can trust Thee. Oh God, come!"

And may it please God now, in prayer, to help some soul to touch Christ and bend the heart to God to come in, and may some souls come to lay this life on Christ at Calvary, and say, "Oh God, given up to the Lord Jesus Christ." Is that blasphemy? No! It is given up in Christ, and Christ lives in me. God will make it a truth and a reality.

Let us pray.

12. The Heavenly Treasure in the Earthen Vessel
(1 Corinthians 4)

In the fourth chapter of second Corinthians and the seventh verse, we have these words:

"But we have this treasure in earthen vessels, that the excellency of the power may be of God and not of us."

Before I begin to speak on the subject direct, let me make two remarks.

The one is that in my first address and later on, I more than once tried to impress the thought that we may be making a great mistake when we seek for the baptism of the Spirit for power for work and service. Not that we are wrong in seeking that. But we are often thinking too exclusively of the power, and not realizing that the Holy Spirit waits to come as a life, renewing our whole being into the likeness of Christ. You know how I have more than once tried to press this side of the truth. Get the Holy Spirit in all His power into your life to make you spiritually minded, to fill you with love and humility, and you will be fitted for work! But I would be very sorry if anyone should think that I count work of little value. All that God wants to do for you has this object: that you may bring forth much fruit. Therefore, beware of misunderstanding me and thinking that I would have you seek only for the higher life. That might be a selfish thing, and therefore I want to speak this morning about work—the work every one of us has to do.

The other remark is this. A good while before I came away from South Africa, I read in an old author a sentence that impressed me deeply and I wrote it down in one of my note books. It was this:

"The first duty of every clergyman is to beg of God, very humbly,
that all that he wants to be done in his hearers may first be fully
and truly done in himself."[167] I cannot say what power there
appears to be in this sentence. Brother minister, and brother
worker, the first duty of one who works for Christ and speaks for
Him is to humbly come to God and ask that everything he wants
done in his hearers may first be thoroughly and fully done in
himself. That brings us to the root of all true work. When I speak
about the love of God, of the power of redemption, of the salvation
from sin, or the filling of the Holy Spirit, or the love of God shed
abroad in the heart, you and I need to have God do the thing in
ourselves—and the more earnestly we seek that, the more there will
be a hidden power of the Holy Spirit to pass through from us, in
whom God has done what He sends us to preach. That thought, I
think you will see, has close connection with the subject we have
this morning.

Paul writes about his ministry, in the first five verses, and then he
says, when he had spoken the wonderful words, "God hath shined
into our hearts, to give us, and through us to give others, the light
of the knowledge of the glory of God in the face of Jesus Christ."[168]
But then he thinks how the Corinthians may despise him, how the
world looked down upon him in all his troubles and humiliation,
and he adds, "But we have this treasure in earthen vessels, that the
excellency of the power may be of God and not of us."[169]

I want to say to all of you—beloved workers, who long to know
what the right spirit is in which to work—that this word is one of
the key words of God about work. It will show you four wondrous
things:

1. The greatness of the heavenly treasure

---

[167] Elsewhere Murray attributes this to William Law
[168] 2 Corinthians 4:6
[169] 2 Corinthians 4:7

2. The feebleness of the earthly vessel

3. The abiding difference between the two

4. The living union in which they are found

1. The greatness of the heavenly treasure

First of all, the heavenly treasure. What is that? You know what he
has stated in the words I have just quoted: "God hath shined into
our hearts."[170] Think of the sun that makes us have all the
sunshine; the sunshine into our eyes, into our bodies, into our very
spirit, and gives warmth and heat and light of life. So Paul says,
"God, the Everlasting One, has shined, and is shining all along into
our hearts." To give what? Shining gives light, and God shining
gives the light of the glory of God. Yes, "the light of the knowledge
of the glory of God in the face of Christ."[171] Does that not bring us
back to what I have said more than once: Christ wants to bring us
to God, and in the face of Christ our one great study, our one great
object and desire should be that the glory of God may be revealed
in us, that we like the angels in heaven walk before Him with
bowed faces, worshiping and adoring all the day long.

God shines into our hearts by the Holy Spirit, and by the Holy
Spirit He reveals the light of the knowledge of the glory of God. It is
not an intellectual knowledge, but in the heart. A man may have
beautiful thoughts, he may be a splendid preacher, he may be a
most edifying instructor, yet there may be very much more of
intellect in him that of God's Spirit. It must be a religion of the
heart. God is love. The love of God is the love of the heart. God
seeks the heart, and God shines into the heart, and in the heart the
seed of love dwells, and the love of God reveals His glory—the light
of the knowledge of the glory of God in the face of Jesus Christ.

---

[170] 2 Corinthians 4:6
[171] Ibid.

Now what is the heavenly treasure I am to have and I am to carry? I may use different words: I can call it the light of God, I can call it the knowledge of God, I can call it the glory of God, I can call it the love of God in Jesus Christ. Dear friends, the treasure you have to carry as a worker for God is a heavenly treasure. The more you realize its greatness, the more you will be able to do your work. If I am a poor man and a beggar asks me for something, I may give him according to what I have. I may give him the last dollar. But if I am rich, I could give him thousands if need be. I can give liberally. Believer, if you get the consciousness, "I am a rich man, I am a millionaire, I have heavenly treasures, I have the key of the treasures of my God," oh, what joy and confidence and power you will have to make others believe there is a heavenly blessing to get!

Oh, we talk about the blessing and try to know the different truth, but how different if our hearts were burning with the heavenly life of God! If the life of God burns in us, in the deepest regions of our being, what a life of blessing! Just think of a life, with the light of the face of the glory of God shining into us all the day! What a heavenly treasure to carry about with us! That light would shine through us and would be reflected from us. I pray you get the light of the glory of God into your souls.

Oh workers, the heavenly treasure is not human knowledge, it is not thought, it is not a little experience, but it is the very sunshine of God's glory in the soul. God would have you take the heavenly treasure, and if you will get your souls full of the consciousness, "I am carrying about the heavenly treasure in me, I am an earthen vessel, but I have the heavenly treasure," you would go forth in new confidence and power.

Oh, study it not only in books, nor even in the Bible! I do not depreciate books; and ten thousand times, no, I do not depreciate the Bible, but the Bible cannot give it you. The Bible is only a pointer to show you up to God that you may be able to come into God's presence. It is found only in God's presence.

Say, "Oh God, shine into my heart." Remember that the shining of God must come ever fresh upon you. I have said, and I will repeat it—I do not weary in repeating it because it is such a lesson: I cannot live on the sunlight of yesterday. I cannot live on the sunlight of an hour ago. I must have the sunlight fresh every moment. And just so this shining of God into our hearts must be the living, unceasing, divine shining of God Himself. Therefore, if the believer wants to be a worker for God, wants to carry the treasure in ever fresh power, his one desire must be to abide every moment in the full light of God's love and God's presence.

Young man and young woman, students of this Bible Institute, I pray you remember: a man has as much real power for eternity as he has of God shining into his heart. And while I pray you to be faithful in your study and use your time well, and while I would urge you use every opportunity for getting acquainted with that precious word, yet I say: first and last, everything depends upon a man living in the light of God's presence, in the light of God's love, and waiting until he has the heavenly treasure in his heart—God shining there the light of the knowledge of the glory of God in the face of Jesus Christ. May every act of faith in Christ lead you up to God, and stir you to wait upon the Everlasting God, to reveal Himself more fully. Let there be a holy hunger and thirst of the heart after God and after a life like that of Christ's, living every hour in fellowship with the Father, and in dependence upon Him.

Oh, what a blessed work the work of the ministry! What a blessed work, proclaiming the salvation of Jesus Christ! The humblest teacher or Bible reader can go to others carrying not only the Bible but the very light of God shining into him and out of him. A lamp is not made to light, but to carry the light; and I carry the light of the knowledge of the glory of God in my heart, carry Jesus Christ Himself, carry the glory of God. Dear brother, the most precious thing you have in your heart, and the most blessed thing you can desire is to have God fill that heart: a heavenly treasure in an earthen vessel.

2. The feebleness of the earthly vessel

Why is it that so many believers and so many workers and so many ministers, enjoy so little of this glory of the heavenly treasure? The answer is simply: because they are all looking at the earthly treasure in a wrong way. Many ministers and Christians are always saying, "I am so weak, I am so feeble, and my thoughts are so poor, and my experience is so wretched," and they do not understand why God puts the treasure in the earthen vessel. They have not accepted their position as an earthen vessel. The more conscious I am of the utter valuelessness of the earthen vessel, the more I can rejoice in the glory of the treasure.

Here on earth people generally seek to have some proportion between the treasure and the vessel in which it is kept. Take the richest people in Chicago, whose wives have received from husbands the most beautiful diamonds and jewellery—we will find them all in beautiful caskets, elegantly polished and made most expensively, some inlaid with gold, some all of gold. We always expect some proportion between the treasure and the vessel, and people think, "according to the beauty of the vessel will be the beauty of the treasure."

God does the very opposite, and that is why Paul says in our text how he was persecuted and had to suffer. It was all well; he knew he was an earthen vessel with a heavenly treasure. The more he felt the insignificance of the earthen vessel, the more he rejoiced in the heavenly treasure. When at Johannesburg, I was shown over a gold mine. Coming out from the door of the furnace room we met a man carrying something in a plain iron vessel. When asked, by the manager to lift the cover, we saw gold to the value of $1,000 being brought in to the furnace. He had that lump of gold in a common iron vessel that you could get for a half a dollar. There was a very precious treasure in a very common vessel. God wants us to realize that. His plan and His delight is to put the heavenly treasure into an earthen vessel. Let us be content with that.

Every one of us has often experienced that, and it has cast us down. You want to preach but feel unable to do as you would wish. You have not the warmth and fullness you like to have. You are cast down because you look in the earthen vessel. Your whole thought should be, "Let the heavenly treasure be magnified." If you are full of that, God will help you to praise Him and your whole heart will be ever set on one thing—the heavenly treasure. God will honor it, and all the time and strength that you have will be saved for the one blessed work of praising God and trusting Him and waiting upon Him. We have a heavenly treasure in an earthen vessel.

Beloved workers, if I could rouse your hearts by the Holy Spirit to consider your position, listen while I tell you: God in heaven has a treasure. Its worth passes all thought, and that treasure is His beloved Son. "In Him it hath pleased the Father that all the fullness should dwell."[172] "In Him are hidden all the riches of the wisdom and of the knowledge of God."[173] Christ is God's treasure and God's delight, and the storehouse of all God's riches. God had that treasure in heaven but sent it down to earth, and in the Babe of Bethlehem, in that Jesus who had not a place to lay His head, in that Jesus as an earthen vessel, there was that heavenly treasure of God. The Jesus that went down into the grave in that broken earthen vessel was the treasure of God. He lifted Him up to the glory, and then the Holy Spirit came down to bring that heavenly treasure into the hearts of men. And the treasure in heaven that God delights in can be a treasure in your heart that you can delight in.

Do let every worker take time to study this. May God show His people—show me—the heavenly treasure that I carry about. The treasure of God's heart is the treasure of my heart. The glory of God shines in the face of His beloved Son; and though you are an earthen vessel, your joy, your confidence and your power may be

---

[172] Colossians 1:19
[173] Colossians 2:3

unfailing. In the earthen vessel we have the heavenly treasure.

3. The abiding difference between the two

There is another point I mentioned. We want to speak about the abiding difference between the two. Some people would think: "Yes, at the beginning of the Christian life, a man will feel that very clearly. It is a very earthen vessel with a heavenly treasure in it. But when a man has been living a spiritual life, living in fellowship with God for years, should he still feel he is just an earthen vessel? When a man has become humble and Christlike, will he then still be an earthen vessel?" Yes, beloved. Paul had been for years in the rich experience of God's grace, and yet he speaks of himself as an earthen vessel. And he would remain one until the end, and why? The reason is given in our text: "That the excellency of the power may be of God."[174]

We are, by nature, so full of pride and self in the most spiritual believer there is always danger of self-exaltation. Remember, in 2 Corinthians 12 Paul writes, "Lest I should be exalted by the revelations I had received, God sent a thorn in the flesh to humble me,"[175] and you know how Christ taught him that when he was weak he would be strongest, because Christ's power would rest upon his weakness.[176] And even so God comes to us. We are ever in danger of beginning to think that we are something; that God is putting this heavenly treasure, ever more abundantly in us. Or when we begin to think that God uses us to dispense to others again the heavenly treasure, and makes us a blessing to others, there is danger of our forgetting what we are; and so God says it shall be forever a heavenly treasure in a mere earthen vessel.

[174] 2 Corinthians 4:7
[175] 2 Corinthians 12:7
[176] 2 Corinthians 12:9

I have pressed you to remember and study what the treasure is, for it is very heavenly. I now press you to study the other side: no matter how many you have brought to Christ, the vessel is still earthen. You are nothing. Oh, if you once begin to understand it, you will not only be content to accept the position but rejoice in it. In regard to this there may be three states of mind:

i. The one is when a man does not want to be an earthen vessel. He longs to be something better—to beautify the vessel by culture and study. He does not want to be an earthen vessel and he is unwearied in the effort to improve the earthen vessel.

ii. It is a step in advance when a man begins to consent to be an earthen vessel. He begins to feel he cannot be otherwise and tries to submit to it. He bears it as a humiliation but does not rejoice in it.

iii. Third step. He begins to delight in being an earthen vessel. He sees why it should be so, and approves of it. He counts it his highest blessedness.

Paul did not get to the position we referred to in 12th chapter of 2 Corinthians at once. When the Lord sent that messenger of Satan to buffet him, he said three times, "Lord, do take it away."[177] The Lord came to Paul and said, "You do not know that the messenger of Satan is your greatest blessing." "Why, Lord?" "Because he will teach you to be absolutely dependent upon Me every moment." Paul got a sight of it: he says, "I will glory, will rejoice in my infirmities, in the weakness of the earthen vessel."[178] That is a higher attainment: not only to endure but to rejoice in being an earthen vessel.

Remember, no matter how full God may fill your heart with His

---

[177] 2 Corinthians 12:8
[178] See 2 Corinthians 12:10

salvation, the consciousness will always have to grow deeper: "I am an earthen vessel." That is why Paul says, in the same chapter, "In nothing am I behind the chiefest of the Apostles, though I am nothing."[179] God made the creature originally to be a vessel in which to show forth His divine glory. This is your highest honor: to be a vessel to carry the power and light of God. That is what angels were created for: to be vessels in which the glory of God could be shown forth. That is what the child of God should be content to be: a vessel—empty, low and broken, if need be—to be filled with Christ, the treasure of God.

4. The living union in which they are found

My last thought. The abiding union between the two—the living union. I said there is an abiding difference to the end. But remember also, there is a living union. There was no living union between that mass of gold away in Johannesburg, I spoke of, and that iron dish. The two were separate. But the treasure of God enters into a man. Though I remain an earthen vessel, the heavenly treasure becomes mine in such a way that it enters my life and becomes myself. All the life of God, and the Holy Spirit of God, and the Holy love of God, and Holy Son of God, and the Holy glory of God, they all—all—pass down into my very being in such an infinite, divine reality, that they are my very own and they make up myself.

God teaches me a double lesson. First of all, to understand the everlasting difference—that I as a creature, ever am nothing but a vessel. If I begin to know the glory of God, I don't want to be anything else; I become jealous of the honor and glory of God and my highest desire is to get lower and deeper down, that God may be all. But with this abiding difference there comes what appears a contradiction, and yet is a blessed reality. I know that the treasure

---

[179] 2 Corinthians 12:11

is not in me and that all my being is only emptiness that holds it, yet this living treasure becomes my very self. This living treasure fills me and becomes inseparably one with me, for my life and for my work.

The heavenly treasure is in the earthen vessel. What is the object? The object is this: that the excellency of the power may be of God. Yes, that is why God has put the heavenly treasure in the earthen vessel—that His beloved servants may learn to be filled with the thought that the power is of God alone. Let my one aim be to be nothing. No being can tell how God will give the heavenly treasure into the heart that is thoroughly empty.

Dear friends, we sum it all up in two thoughts. The one: beloved child of God be very humble and get very low down. The other: beloved child of God, be very trustful and get very high up.

I have said it more than once: be very humble. Young men and young women who are studying, I pray you, by the mercies of God, whatever you study do not forget to study humility. Someone has said, "pray to be delivered from every vestige of pride, as spirits in torment would pray if they had any hope of being delivered."[180] Pray to be delivered from every secret root of anything like pride. Pray to be brought down to the dust before your God. Take time to get low before God. God giveth grace to the humble. If you want to get the heavenly treasure, get low. A vessel must be empty, clean and lowly. Let us all be willing to say, "Lord, deepen in my soul the conviction of my utter nothingness, and let me walk in holy fear and trembling," and let it be one desire of my heart to get low enough before God that God may fill me.

The other thought: Be very trustful and rise high in your expectation. I bring you this message; you want to be workers. I might have spoken about the love we need for souls, and the glory

---

[180] Elsewhere Murray attributes this to William Law

of God in our work, and about prayer in work—but here is the chief thing, Christian worker: be very trustful. God has a treasure: His beloved Son. God hath entrusted you who are believers with this treasure. It is in your heart. You can hide it, you can hinder it, or you can open your being very wide to be filled with it. Oh, do believe in the glory of that treasure, in the power of that treasure, in the heavenly joy of that treasure, in its unutterable riches? It is God shining into you His sunshine, His love—God shining His Spirit, God shining His love into your very heart.

Begin to open your heart very wide, and so every moment of the day let the treasure come in. Every moment of the day let God shine into your heart the glory of His Son, and believe you will be able to say with Paul, "We have this treasure."[181] Let us say today, "I have this treasure—this divine treasure—and I am going to ask my God to reveal it to me." I walk tremblingly at the thought: I carry the heavenly treasure. If you had a diamond of twenty thousand dollars, how carefully you would keep it!

Believers, don't be so occupied with your work for Christ and study as to forget the chief thing: "I have the heavenly treasure. Let me walk carefully and watchfully, believing God alone will keep shining all the time." May every heart here know what it is: every hour, every moment, God shines into me the light of the knowledge of the glory of God in the face of Christ.

> Moment by moment I'm kept in His love,
> Moment by moment I've life from above.[182]

God shines it and keeps it shining as He does the sunlight.

---

[181] 2 Corinthians 4:7
[182] *Moment By Moment* by D W Whittle

13. Yield Yourselves unto God[183]
(Romans 6:13)

It is of great consequence that we keep very clearly before our eyes what the object of our gathering is. We look at the state of God's Church, at the great majority of Christians, and hear them complain of their feebleness and continual failure, and we want to ask the question, "Is there not, in God's word, sufficient provision to enable a child of God to live a spiritual, humble life of victory all along the line?"

We want to ask this question regarding our selves. So many of us have to say, "I know that Christ is an Almighty Savior. That I believe. But He does not prove to be an Almighty Savior to me." Is that not the position toward God many of us occupy? There are elementary truths that we think we can live by. What there is in God's word for making strong Christians has been too often regarded as applicable to the few who we think are called to a special service. And so many want to get all the religion and happiness they can with as little of sacrifice as possible. They don't understand that just as a man who wants to come out first in an examination or to take a good place in a profession or business must go at it with his whole heart and give his time and strength to it, so religion requires a man to give up everything to know God in Christ.

Your first business is to be a man of God as God wants you to be. You will never regret it. We cannot be first-rate, thoroughgoing Christians without giving a great deal of concentrated, intense attention to it, and waiting on God to make us as Christ was. Christ

---

[183] This chapter and Chapter 14 are the other way around in the original printed edition, but it's clear from references in the text that this is the correct order.

did not become what He was without giving up everything. The twelve apostles had to give up everything. Dear friends, if we give up ourselves entirely to God's training then we can become strong Christians.

When I look upon the state of the church in England and elsewhere, I feel sure that God will have to call out a number of people to separate themselves from everything—give themselves up entirely just as Jesus did—to get the fullest possible experience of the love and will of God. Through such men God will be able to bless His other children. God comes to this company with the question, "Are you desirous to be and to do and to have the very utmost that God can give you?" There are some hearts who say, "Yes."

I invite you to listen to a portion of God's word that you all know. You will find the words in Romans 6:13. Bible students know that this text is found in the second of the four great divisions of the Epistle to the Romans. The first division from 1:16 to 5:11—righteousness by faith. The second division is from Chapter 5:12 to the end of Chapter 8—life by faith. Third division, Chapters 9, 10 and 11—the mystery of faith; the deep mystery of God's purpose and council with mankind. And then from Chapter 12 to the end you have the walk of faith.

Now, here we have the life of faith. You know the words in Habakkuk that Paul takes as the text of his Epistle, "The just shall live by faith."[184] Faith gives two things: faith gives righteousness and faith gives life. These two things have been separated in the first part of the Epistle. Paul begins by explaining the righteousness of faith, how we are justified. Then he points out what the ground is of that justification by faith, and that is our living union with Christ.

---

[184] Habakkuk 2:4

People often ask, "Is it right in God to take Christ and lay our sin upon Him, and to take me, the guilty one, and pardon for the sake of One who died?" God does not justify me for the righteousness of Christ as long as I have no part in it. Christ is one body with me; I am in Him by faith. He becomes vitally connected with me. We don't count it strange if we take a twig from a tree or seed and plant it, that the tree that springs from it is of the same nature. So, it is not strange that when Adam fell and died, I should share his sin. It is most natural. And so, if Christ and I are one it is not strange that God should justify me in Christ. But the believer must not only know that he is justified but must know that he is in Christ.

Chapter 5:12. Paul begins his great argument to prove how we have not only righteousness, but life in Christ. Just as we died in Adam, so we may live in Christ; those who receive the gift of righteousness, they reign in life; from Christ they have not only pardon and acceptance, but victory; they are not only saved, but made kings unto God. After having laid this foundation in the second part of Chapter 5, he goes on in Chapter 6 to explain this further—to tell us the only way to conquer sin is to know our union with Christ.

Justification does not deal with the question, "How I can conquer sin?" but deals with the question, "How can I be delivered from past sin and get right with God?" It is quite another question, "How am I to conquer sin?" His answer is, "Shall we sin that grace may abound? God forbid. How shall we who are dead to sin live any longer there in?"[185] Paul says, "Know you not that when you were baptized into Christ you were baptized into His death?"[186] You were made partakers of His death. You were united with Him in the likeness of His death, therefore reckon yourselves as indeed dead to sin. You are dead to sin because you are one with the Christ who died to sin.

---

[185] Romans 6:2
[186] Romans 6:3

You say to an unconverted man, "You are dead in sin; you are dead to God." How did he become dead? He died. How did he die? He died in Adam. Every one of us died in Adam, and the life that we get from Adam is dead to God. Just so, when I believe in Christ, I get a life in Christ dead to sin—the very life of Christ who died on Calvary. That life—dead to sin, raised up by the glory of God—that life is in me. And Paul says you have got to believe that until your whole heart becomes full of it and cries out, "Praise God, I am dead to sin; the living Christ is in me, I am alive unto God in Christ Jesus."

After having expounded this, Paul says, "Reckon, count, yourselves dead—actually dead—dead to sin; for you are dead, and alive unto God in Christ Jesus."[187] Then follows, "Therefore"—what must be the result? "Let not sin therefore reign in you." You have done with sin—you are dead to sin.

"Let not sin any more reign in your mortal body." You are dead to sin; but your body is not dead yet and sin can tempt you, and though you are dead to sin you can be tempted and mastered through the body. So, yield your members to God and let the Holy Spirit mortify the deeds of the body.

"Let not sin reign in your mortal body." Why is it believers let sin reign in their mortal bodies? Because they do not understand or accept this truth in Romans 6:11: "You are dead to sin and alive to God."

"Let not sin reign in your mortal body." "Nor yield your members." You have got the power of Christ's life in you; don't yield your lives to unrighteousness, or "your members as instruments of unrighteousness unto sin". Now comes my text: "But yield yourselves unto God as alive from the dead, and your members as instruments of righteousness unto God."

---

[187] The following paragraphs closely expound Romans 6:11-13

If the believer wants to know what is the position he has to take before God to know whether he can conquer sin, he will find it in these words: "Present yourselves unto God as alive from the dead, and present your members as instruments of righteousness unto God."[188] Paul will show in the seventh chapter that even when I am dead to sin I may be tempted to get into a legal state, and by self-effort and self-struggling may begin trying to fulfill the law—but it will be utter failure. He will then take us on to the eighth chapter and will show us that by the Holy Spirit all that is taught in Chapters 6 and 7 can be made a reality to us, and that the Holy Spirit will make the death and life of Christ a living reality.

So, our great need is to be freed by the Spirit from the law of sin and death, and also led by it to mortify the deeds of the body. But if we want it made clear to us how we are to live that blessed life in the Spirit, we must first understand what it means, "Yield yourselves unto God." "Present yourselves as alive from the dead." In speaking on these words, I wish to answer three questions: Who? How? Why?

1. Who?

Who are to do this, to present themselves unto God as alive from the dead? This is the lesson: "Present yourselves unto God as alive from the dead."[189] A man can truly present or yield himself to God only as he knows he is alive from the dead. If a man thinks he is a Christian but that the larger part of his nature is sin, that there is a little spark of life amid a mass of what is sinful, he cannot make a proper presentation of himself to God. The secret and the strength of your yielding yourself to God lies in this: "I am alive from the dead."

---

[188] Romans 6:13
[189] Romans 6:11

Many people trouble themselves greatly to apprehend intellectually
the expression, "Dead to sin and alive unto God in Christ Jesus."[190]
Let us far rather accept it in the faith that God knows its full
meaning and obey the injunction of our text, to present ourselves
to God as alive from the dead. You can understand that if I am alive
from the dead then it is no more than right—and indeed the only
right thing—that I should say, "Lord, I have got this life from Thee;
I cannot keep it or maintain it; I come to Thee with it." However
much of darkness or ignorance, dear believer, do come and say,
"Lord God, this is all Thy life; Thou hast given it me to Christ; it is
Thine own life, I present it unto Thee; I yield myself unto Thee as
alive from the dead."

"Present yourselves unto God!" You know what I said yesterday
morning about Christ bringing us unto God. That is the same thing
in another form. The whole object of Christ's work is to bring us
near to God. And the first thing the apostle gives us to do—when he
has taught us how, after dying with Christ, we have been raised
with Him—is to come with this new life and bring it unto God. The
object for which Christ died was to get us very near to God and into
fellowship with Him.

"Present yourselves unto God!" How often have I to do it? It must
be every moment. It must become a habit of my life. I have to do it
every day, until the consciousness takes possession of me, I have a
divine life from God; I bring it to God because God does not give
me life in myself that I can have as a possession, that I have as my
own, but as His life working in me, only so far as I yield to Him and
abide in communion with Him.

Ye who are alive from the dead, "present yourselves unto God!" Do
it every day until your whole soul is filled with the living faith of
your true position. The everlasting God has begun a life in me and
is carrying it on every moment of the day. Every moment I can

---

[190] Ibid.

count that God will maintain it. Don't you see that we have been too much guilty of breaking off the connection with God, and our life is in broken communion? If I can learn to walk all the day in God's presence, presenting myself unto Him as alive from the dead, God will make the resurrection-life of Christ to work in me day and night, secretly, quietly, gently, and effectively.

You that are justified, you that know you have life in Christ, "present yourselves unto God!" Everything must come from Him. We now know who are those who have to do it—those that are alive from the dead. What are the marks of those that are alive? God's life is no mere imagination, thought, conception; it is a great reality. Remember that this life must bear two marks: it is a life that has been dead, and a life that is now alive from the dead. These are the marks of Christ's life in heaven. In Revelation He says, "I am He that liveth and was dead, and am alive for evermore."[191] The life of Christ in glory is ever a life from the dead. In heaven they ever sing the song of the Lamb and the praise of His blood.[192] If the death and the life are linked together there, it must be so too in the believer here. There must be the mark of death and the mark of life.

What are the marks of death? The death marks of Jesus, the disposition which took Him to death, we know. Humility. He humbled Himself and gave Himself up to death. Humility is one of the death marks in the believer. Death to sin, separation from all sin, is another mark. Another death mark is separation from the world, to be crucified to the world. Then there is deep impotence, helplessness. When Christ went down into the grave, He was helpless. And this is perfect restfulness. He rested in the grave in hope. In the believer who is really dead in Christ you will find these marks.

---

[191] Revelation 1:18
[192] Revelation 5

i. You will find very deep humility. I am nothing but a redeemed sinner, nothing but a creature in whom God can work His glory. It was humility that led Christ to the death, and humility will be the death mark in everyone that has died in Christ Jesus.

ii. Separation from all sin. Christ died to sin—died rather than yield to sin. An intense desire to be free from every sin; the readiness to give up life rather than sin; counting all things but loss to be made conformable to His death, are the marks of a life that roots in the death of Christ.

iii. Separation from the world. A man feels, "I belong to another sphere; I am living in eternity; I am living with God; I am separate from the world; I may have to do my work because I am in the world, but I am not of the world as Christ was not of the world."

iv. Along with that, another mark is impotence—nothing of self-effort. We ever try to do something of ourselves instead of taking our place at the foot of the throne so that God can work in us. The deeper the Spirit of Christ's death enters us, the more we shall be willing to be nothing, that God may be and may work all.

v. The last mark is restfulness. In the grave Jesus rested. He gave up His Spirit and rested in the grave. The death mark of the believer is deep restfulness. Jesus knew God would fulfill His work. As the believer advances, he learns to rest perfectly in his God.

On the other side, let us look at the life marks.

i. The first life mark is victory. Jesus has conquered death and hell, and "we are more than conquerors through Him that loved us".[193]

ii. Another life mark is joy. It was "for the joy that was set before

---

[193] Romans 8:37

Him He endured the cross".[194] Deliverance gives joy. If we would be filled with the resurrection joy, the joy of triumph over sin and death, we have it in Christ. It is ours because we are alive from the dead. Resurrection life is in us. The living Christ is living in us. How little is the joy of the world compared to the deep joy of redemption filling our souls!

iii. Another mark is the power of blessing. The Lord Jesus rose from the dead and began to bless. The first night He breathed His Spirit upon the disciples.[195] On the day of His resurrection there was blessing, and in the outpouring of His Spirit this dispensation became one of divine, infinite blessing. If you are living in Christ, your resurrection life will be one of blessing to others.

"Present yourselves unto God," all that are alive from the dead! Present yourself by the Holy Spirit and ask God to make the death marks more clear and the life marks more beautiful, and your whole life will be from God and before God as of those alive from the dead. Say, "I have died. I have been crucified with Christ. God has raised me." And the more intensely you present yourselves to God in that life, the more intensely will it manifest itself in your daily life. A life out of death, a life of victory, the resurrection life in Christ will be yours in truth. You will begin to walk before God as one alive from the dead. With Christ I go down into the grave, give up myself as lost; God raises me up in Christ and makes me alive from the dead.

Yield up yourselves, believers, to know Christ! You are alive from the dead—accept it in faith. Yield yourselves, present yourselves unto God.

2. How?

---

[194] H3ebrews 12:2
[195] John 20:22

Second question: How are we to do this? Note here very carefully how the apostle answers it. He makes a difference between myself and my members. He says, "Yield yourselves unto God as those that are alive from the dead, and your members as instruments of righteousness unto God." What is that difference? We find in the sixth, seventh and eighth chapters, the difference occurs continually between the new life, the renewed self, and the body or the members.

Sin is continually represented as having power in the members of the believer after he himself has been made alive from the dead; so Paul says in Romans 7, "In me, that is in my flesh, dwelleth no good thing. If I do that which I would not it is not I, but sin, that dwelleth in me."[196] Paul speaks of the center of his life as the renewed "I." The "I" has been regenerated. The "I" is alive now in Christ. It is that "I" of which he says: "I have died to sin, I am alive to God. It is not I but sin." That new "I" dwells in the body with its members. Sin is in my flesh, so I find the law of sin in my members that leads me into captivity to the law of sin and death. It is a saved man who says, "I delight in the law of God after the inward man."[197] It is not I who sins—my will utterly loathes the sin—but this body of death is full of sin. I am impotent and am taken captive. And then Paul says the reason is that he was trying to obey the law in his own strength but failed.

This leads me on to Chapter 8, where you get at once the deliverance of the Holy Spirit who personally works in you what Christ has done and sets you free from the law of sin and death in your members and enables you, through the Spirit, to mortify the deeds of the body. It is in this sense he says, "Yield yourself unto God as alive from the dead, and your members as instruments of righteousness unto God." He does not say the members are alive from the dead. You as the living one are to present them to God.

---

[196] Romans 7:18,20
[197] Romans 7:22

You ask how you are to bring your members into subjection, to yield them as instruments of righteousness unto God. I must not only try as a spiritual man to say, "Lord, here is my self, my inmost heart and love"; but I must take my members, my flesh, my body, in which is the power of sin, and I must say, "Lord, these members I give up to Thee as instruments of righteousness."

Before Paul comes to the beautiful teaching of the first part of Chapter 7, he wants you to take up this word. From the 16th verse of the sixth chapter he amplifies it in a very practical passage of the utmost importance. In it the three words are found: righteousness, obey, service. These words occur repeatedly. The lesson is this: After you have accepted the first half of Romans 6 there is a great deal of spiritual teaching in Romans 7 and 8, to which you are to be led on. But in between he introduces this practical parenthesis: if you are alive from the dead, if you have yielded yourselves to God, begin at once and take these three words and bring them into practice.

i. Righteousness. You have been declared righteous by God that you may live in practical righteousness upon earth. Be careful. If you are going to live as alive from the dead, do not sin. Do not ask the question, "How far can I go and not sin?", but take simply what God says, "Sin not." Say, "I am going to live for the highest righteousness." Righteousness is the very foundation of God's throne; it must be so too in the Christian life. Do not seek beautiful spiritual thoughts and experiences when you speak of being dead and alive in Christ, but come at once and yield every member to be nothing but an instrument of righteousness.

ii. There is the second word: serve. You are to be the servant of righteousness. A man can sometimes be in the position of a servant and yet act as if he were master. We need the deep conviction, "I have been delivered from the service of sin to become a servant of God and His righteousness." As we yield ourselves to God daily it must be with the one desire: to keep the place of servants before

Him. Our Jesus took the form of a servant. That was His life, and made Him the Father's delight. That must be our Spirit.

iii. One word more. I have sometimes got a favorite servant who works hard but often works in his own way instead of carefully obeying my will. Remember, you are not only to live as a servant but as one who obeys, who waits daily upon God to find out His will and who works righteousness, not according to his own but according to God's thoughts.

If you walk in the path you will understand the answer to the question, "How am I to present myself?" You will yield yourselves, your inmost being, as renewed in Christ, as alive from the dead unto God, and bring your members each time and present each one of them—each power and movement of your being—to God as an instrument of righteousness. And your inner life with God will be manifested in your conversation among men.

3. Why?

Last question. Why ought we thus to present ourselves to God and our members as instruments of righteousness? I can only very hastily say a few words on this. Let it be a presentation of thanksgiving, dear believer. Every time you think of it—"I am alive from the dead"—let your heart rise up with wonderful thanksgiving. Present yourself unto God. Yield your body, soul, and spirit a living sacrifice. Is that not a privilege, an unspeakable honor? You may walk in the sunshine of God's love with God, in the gladness that says, "I offer myself just out of deep gratitude for the life of Christ. I am alive from the dead." Oh beloved, if you would have the joy of God's heaven in your heart, praise Him for the wonderful mystery of the resurrection of Christ in you! You dead with Christ and alive with Christ, present yourselves to God in praise!

Present yourself in surrender. I am not my own; I have been

bought with the blood; I have been paid for; I present myself as belonging to God. Christ suffered that He might bring us to God. Christ died; we died with Him; God made us alive with Him, that we might serve God. Give yourself up in absolute surrender. Have nothing in your members, your conduct, your temper, that is not entirely subjected to the life of God. Bring all every day to God, that by His Holy Spirit the death in Christ may be fully manifested in you. Bring everything you have, dear friends—your mind, your power of thought, your heart, your love, your joy; bring everything and lay it before God. Have you ever thought of Jesus after God had raised Him from the dead? If He had turned away from heaven and gone to live in the world, what would have become of us? Shall we do it? Shall we dare to do it—to live worldly lives, to live sinful lives? Shall we do it after we have been raised from the dead? Shall we not say, "I present myself to God, that He do with me only what pleases Him."

Let it not only be a presentation of thanksgiving and surrender, but also one of holy spiritual expectancy. I said at the beginning in regard to this life from the dead, that we do not know how to keep it or maintain it. But if God has begun the work, He will continue it. If He has given it, He will maintain it. The life God bestowed in resurrection, He will perfect. He waits for you every day to present yourself as alive from the dead; to bring every member as an instrument of righteousness, and to have large expectations of what your God will do for you.

Do believe with your whole heart, my brother, that God is able and willing to lead you to live upon earth as a living Lazarus—raised from the dead by the mighty power and to the glory of God. He can enable you every day to live the resurrection life. Do believe that! Only remember this: you must in Christ present yourself every day to God in holy expectancy, waiting for Him to work in you, waiting on Him in faith to answer prayer in which you express your surrender to God.

This brings me back in closing to where we were yesterday morning. Christ suffered that He might bring us unto God. Let this be your one object as you reckon yourselves as alive from the dead—dead to self and alive with Jesus; let it be your one object to get near to God. We want more time in secret prayer if the resurrection life is to work in power; more time alone with God for God to perfect His work in me.

Believer, yield yourself unto God. Let your life bear the stamp. Ask God to write it in your heart: "a God-yielded man, a God-devoted man," that God may perfect the life He began in Christ. It will be a life of victory, of joy, of blessing, to live as a God-yielded man, waiting continually upon God to work His work perfectly in you.

Let us believe that all this is indeed for each one here. Shall we not trust God by His Holy Spirit to make it true? He uses the words of the speaker. They may be feeble, but He uses even these thoughts to make His own precious word true in actual reality in our souls.

Shall we not trust God for it? Shall we not trust God that the Holy Spirit does set us free from the law of sin and death in our members; that the Holy Spirit does give us strength to mortify the deeds of the body, so that our lives shall indeed be as those walking in Christ and walking in the Spirit?—monuments of the power of God who quickened the dead, and makes us conformable to His blessed Son.

14. Willing and Doing
(Romans 7:18, Philippians 2:12-13)

The words of my text this evening you find in Romans and Philippians. Romans, the seventh chapter, the second half of the 18th verse:

> *"For to will is present with me, but how to perform that which is good, I know not."*

And then Philippians, the second chapter and the 12th verse, the second half, and the 13th:

> *"Work out your own salvation with fear and trembling, for it is God which worketh in you, both to will and to do of His good pleasure."*

You see how these two texts appear to contradict one another. The first text gives us the experience of a man who says, "To will is present with me—my will is right; I am willing to do God's will; I am willing to do what is good. But," he says, "I have not the power. How to perform I find not." It is a man with whom there is a great gulf between willing and doing. Just the state of a great many Christians. They will what is good, and somehow they have not the strength to perform. They cannot understand it themselves, and others cannot understand it, and yet it is exactly as you have it here. "To will is present with me, but how to perform I find not." In the second text you have the very opposite. There Paul says, "Work out your own salvation with fear and trembling, for it is God which worketh in you, both to will and to do according to His good pleasure." Here is a man in whom Paul says that God does both the things: not only the willing but the doing also.

Now in these two texts we have just the exact description of the two stages of the Christian life that I have been speaking about so repeatedly. You know when we began, last Tuesday, to speak about the carnal and spiritual, I pointed out that there are two styles of Christian living. The one is that of the carnal Christian, who tries to be good but can't succeed. He always fails. Temper and strife and sin get the better of him. The other is the spiritual Christian, who gets the victory. Just so here. There are people who are always complaining. "Oh, I do desire to please God; it is my will and purpose to do His will, but I can't do it." They have not the strength. But there are other Christians, to whom Paul's words to the Philippians come as a reality. God works, not only to *will*, but He also works to *do* in them.

Let us try to find out what the difference is between these two states; what the reason is that so many continue in the former state; what the way is to get out of it into the second. Dear friends, don't you see clearly how much better the second life is than the first? A man always willing but not succeeding in doing, or a man both willing and doing—which is best? Every heart can give the answer. Let every heart pray, "God reveal to me how I can get into this blessed life—willing and doing, both."

The first stage: willing but not doing

Now, in speaking about this first stage, I just want to remind you of the place that the teaching in Chapter 7 has in the Epistle to the Romans. This morning we had the sixth chapter and we saw that Paul says there, to every believer, "You are dead in Christ, you are alive in Christ, you must believe it and reckon upon it and then come and present yourself to God." But that is only the beginning of the work of sanctification. He goes on in the end of the chapter to tell them, "Now begin at once and work that out; live for righteousness, as servants of righteousness, obeying God in everything."

In the seventh chapter he tells them there is something more. After a man begins to try and obey God and live as God's servant in the performance of righteousness, he comes to an unexpected experience: he finds that he fails; and so Paul, in the beginning of the seventh chapter, says to him, "I have to tell you of something more and something better: you are not only dead to sin— everybody can understand that that ought to be—but you are actually dead to the law." The Christian answers, "The law is good and holy, how can I be dead to the law?" Paul tells him the law is indeed good and spiritual; but the law is unfitted for your state because you are sinful by nature and you cannot keep the law, and so the law just kills you. Your mistake in the Christian life after your conversion is this: you try to keep the law and you always fail.

The law was given by God at Sinai to stir men up to their highest activity and urge them to do their very best, that they might learn that they must fail and that they were utterly impotent. That was the work of the law—to convince men of their sinfulness. The believer, when he thinks, "I am a regenerate man, I must try and keep the law," always fails, because the law always calls you to self-effort; it stirs up self, and when self does its best it can do nothing. And so, Paul here in the seventh chapter tells us, "You are not only dead to sin, as I told you in the sixth chapter, but you are actually dead to the law." He then goes on to teach us more about this.

I want you, as you study the Epistle carefully, to note the teaching of the second half of the seventh chapter. In the first division of the Epistle that I spoke of this morning (chapters 1:18 to 5:11), Paul had spoken about sins—sins in the plural, sinful acts—as transgressions, and justification had to do with them. But from the fifth chapter and the twelfth verse he does not talk any more about sins in the plural, but all about sin—S-I-N. Why?

In the first half of the Epistle, when he was talking about

justification, there he had to speak about sinful deeds, but here in the second half he is about to speak of the power of sin that works in us, and how that power is to be conquered. That is the reason why in the second half of the seventh chapter, we enter on a new discussion of the subject of sin.

The Epistle would have been terribly discouraging if we had not had this seventh chapter. Some people are troubled about it, but I thank God exceedingly for it. What would it have helped me if Paul had, in the first chapter, told me all about sin—the sins of the heathen and the sins of the Jews, and pardon and justification in the blood of Christ, dying for our sins—but had not told me about the power of sin in my own life? What would it have helped me if Paul had only told me about the sins of the unconverted man? As a believer, I want to know, "How about the sin of the converted man, sin in the regenerate man?" And therefore, the second half of Romans 7 is indispensable to a right knowledge of the will of God. It teaches us the precious lesson of our impotence, as the way to full deliverance.

I spoke in one of the addresses about there being needed two convictions of sin: a conviction of sin for the unconverted man to bring him to repentance and faith, and for the believer a conviction of sin and sinfulness to prepare him for full salvation. That is the apostle's teaching here in the second half of the seventh chapter. Dear friends, if you read it carefully, you will see that Paul is speaking there about the Christian who is a regenerate man, who delights in the law of God, longs to do what is right and good, and yet is not able. And why not? The answer is, simply because he has not yielded to the Holy Spirit to work within him.

Notice in Chapter 7, from the seventh verse, the name of Christ is not once mentioned except down at the very verse before the last, "I thank God through Jesus Christ our Lord."[198] Notice, the Holy

---

[198] Romans 7:25 (in fact, the last verse of the chapter)

Spirit is not mentioned. Notice, the man is speaking always about the law. The word law occurs from twenty to thirty times. The man is always speaking about I and me. It is a regenerate man doing his very best to keep the law of God, but he fails utterly. That is just the life of the multitude of believers. They are sometimes doing their very best—trying hard, praying and crying to God, "Lord help me!"—but it does not help.

What a change comes in the eighth chapter. Paul begins in the second verse—the law, the dominion of the Spirit, of "the life in Christ has set me free from the dominion of sin and death." That is it! A new power comes in. The power of the Holy Ghost to enable a man not only to will, but to do the will of God. That is the transition from the first state to the second state.

The second stage: both willing and doing

This second state you find described in Philippians 2, verses 12 and 13:

> *"Work out your own salvation with fear and trembling for it is God which worketh in you both to will and to do."*

I remember being very much struck by hearing a young missionary at the Cape, when he was preparing to leave the congregation from which we were sending him out, tell of something that had comforted him much. I think it was in a life of David Brainerd. He had read that when he had resolved to go to the mission field, someone said, "Well, you are very willing to go, aren't you? Yes, but how do you know that you will succeed? How do you know that you will be able to hold out and that you won't turn back?" And his answer was this: "Well, the God who has given the will will give the power to perform it." He works to will and to do. That is all we need to have in the Christian life.

That is what I want to speak about tonight. That the same God who has given the power to will will also give the power to do, so that a Christian need not always live complaining, "I will, I will, but how to perform, I do not find." God will bring a man to the place where, by the living power of the Holy Ghost, he can do God's will and obey God's command. And that is the life we want.

In Romans 7 we have, as we said, the language of the renewed will. Some people think that it refers to the unregenerate will. I cannot think that–the language is far too strong. In the first place, why should he introduce the condition of the unregenerate man between the sixth and eighth chapters, where he is entirely dealing with sanctification? It would be out of place. He is talking about sanctification and why should he put in this passage about the unregenerate man? I cannot think it. But it is in its right place if he comes to tell me what is of far more interest to me than the state of the unconverted man—if he comes to tell me how things are in the heart of the converted man, this is exactly what I need to know. Therefore, I take my text, "To will is present with me, but to perform I find not,"[199] as the language of the regenerate man, and I want to give you some simple lessons which I think these words teach us.

And the first lesson is:

1. The renewed will teaches me the power of regeneration—that God changes the heart and the will and the life and the desire of a man

He turns right from them, and the man who has loved sin, who has not loved God's will and God's law—a man who has loved himself and his own will and done it—that man is changed entirely and he begins to delight in the will of God. I am going to speak to you

---

[199] Romans 7:18

about the impotence and insufficiency of that renewed will tonight, but before I do that I want to magnify that renewed will as the gift of the Everlasting God, and I want to say to you, thank God, if you can honestly say, "Lord, with my whole heart I have purposed and sworn to do that will."[200] Never mind if you fail, never mind if you haven't got the strength to do it yet, but hold on and say to God, "Lord, I delight in Thy will, I delight to do it and I want to do it."[201]

The renewed will teaches me the power of regeneration. You find men trying to change their own hearts, to change their own wills, to change their inclinations, but they have found that they could not change it. But God changes it. I have read the story of a Christian woman losing her temper week after week, and going to her bedroom and praying and crying to God for deliverance, and telling how she did it for years and no deliverance came. The will was right—it has been so with many. That was evidence that God's work was in them, that they did not sit down with the thought, "Well, never mind, there is no great harm." But they never get rest in it. Their will was set upon doing the will of God, though they utterly failed in performing it. And therefore, I say to you, my fellow Christians: though you have not attained yet to the doing of God's will, begin and hold fast that and say, "I will what God wills." Say that. In affliction say—even though your heart trembles and you cannot submit; though you cannot bring your heart to do what you want and to be perfectly submissive—say, "Lord, I will what Thou willest. I give up my will and I choose Thy will, though my heart refuses to rest." Or, with regard to any sin that is troubling you and conquering you, say it to God, "Lord, I will to do what Thou hast commanded." This is my first lesson. The renewed will in my text teaches me the power of regeneration.

But it teaches me in the second place:

---

[200] Possibly from Psalm 119:106
[201] From Psalm 40:8

2. The impotence and powerlessness of the regenerate man

Regeneration gives a man a new will, but the regenerate man after
he has got the new will is an impotent thing. And the great mischief
in our churches and among our Christians is that they don't know
that. People think, "Well, I am regenerate and I have the grace of
God in me and I have got somewhat of God's Spirit in me and I
ought to be able to do God's will," and they try and do their very
best, and they fail. But here comes now the important lesson about
the second blessing and the higher life—or the spiritual life, or
whatever name you call it by—that God comes and tells the
regenerate man: "My son, I have given you a new will, but that new
will alone cannot help you."

Many a man thinks, "If I were only fixed and firm in my will, I
would be able to obey God." He groans and cries to God about it.
He delights in the law of God and yet he cannot do what he wants
to do. Does that not teach me clearly that a regenerate man is an
impotent man? Do I not see it every day of my life? And are there
not a hundred witnesses in this building tonight who can say it is
so? There are some things that a man can't do; there are some
things that he can't forsake. When you come to the daily
temptations of the inner life, the regenerate man is an impotent
man. There are men who for thirty or forty years have fought
against their temper and never conquered it, and they have
admitted it with grief. There are men who have fought for thirty or
forty years against self-will and unlovingness and they have never
conquered it. Why? Because the regenerate man is an impotent
man as long as he tries, in virtue of his regeneration, to serve God.

Then comes my third thought:

3. That the regenerate man, if he is actually to do God's will, needs a new blessing

Needs a new blessing! Yes, that is the great truth which the eighth chapter of Romans teaches us. Paul, in the seventh chapter, is silent about the Spirit—not a word about it. All about the law and the regenerate man who is under the law still, trying to obey the law. But then he comes in the eighth chapter and says, "Not the law, the power of the Spirit of life in Christ hath set me free from that law which took me captive and which prevented my doing what I really willed to do." He says, "The Spirit of Christ does set me free." In Chapter 7, I have a man who is a captive; in Chapter 8, a man who has been set at liberty by God's Spirit.

He goes on to tell me that the Spirit of Christ enables me to walk after the Spirit. By the Spirit I can mortify the deeds of the body so that I do not do any longer what I do not want to. Oh, the blessedness of knowing there is a second step! That second step need not be long after conversion. It sometimes comes with conversion, when the Holy Spirit comes very mightily down upon a man and he at once begins to will and to do. But in the church as it is now, in most cases it does not come at once; and therefore we must preach to you, beloved brethren, that there is a different stage from that on which most of us live. And what is that stage? That stage is when the Holy Spirit comes and fills the heart and a man believes not only "God does work in me to will" but "God will work in me to do."

Oh, the difference between the willing and doing! Take a child. You give a child a sum in arithmetic—a little boy of ten—and he is so willing and he does work so hard and he does his very best. The will is not wanting but he can't do it. Ah, that is just the will of most Christians; you have not the power—you cannot do it. We learn here from Paul in Chapter 7 that the man of whom he speaks hasn't it. But I can say something else. Oh my brother, the Holy Spirit is the mighty power of God for doing, and if you will come and begin to say, "My whole life must be entirely given up to the Spirit of God, and I must allow the Spirit of God to take the place that I, with my own strength, have been trying to take. My whole life must be one of waiting upon the Spirit of God and rejoicing in Him," then God will give not only to will, but to do also. Glory to God's name! Let us depend upon it and believe it and rejoice in it. "It is God which worketh in you both to will and to do."[202]

You ask me, perhaps, why has God arranged it so that there are to be two separate stages, the willing and the doing? Wouldn't it have been better and more blessed if God, when He gave the will had given me the do at the same time? Why did not God give it to that man in Romans 7? There is a divine reason for it and that reason is this: when an unconverted man comes to Christ and God asks that man, "Will you live to do My will?" The unconverted man cannot answer the question, because he does not understand what God's will is. He is blind. He thinks he knows what God's will is, but he cannot in his unconverted state know what the depth and purity of God's will is, and how the will of God reaches to the inmost being. A man, at conversion, cannot yet give a fully intelligent answer to the question. He does not know what it means when he says, "Lord, I will do all Thou sayest."

Israel, at Mount Sinai, said, "All that the Lord hath spoken, we will do," but they did not know what they were saying. Just so, when an unconverted man comes to conversion, he does not know what the will of God is. But after he is converted, then God gives him time— a year, or two years, or three years—and as a regenerate man he begins earnestly to try and do God's will. As a rule, he fails utterly. Then God comes and deals with him a second time, and He says, "My child, I gave you a new will to love My will and you thought you were able to do it; I want to cure you now entirely of self and self-confidence; I have allowed you to try your best and you have seen how you have utterly failed in the doing of my will. Come now, a second time, and let me give you a new blessing." And if he asks, "Father, what is this blessing? Hast Thou not given me the Holy Spirit?" God answers, "Yes, thou art a temple of the Spirit and the Spirit is in thee, but thou hast never understood what it is to have

---

[202] Philippians 2:13

thy whole being entirely filled with the Spirit. Thou hast never understood what it is, all the day and every day to be entirely dependent upon the Holy Spirit. Thou hast never understood how fully and entirely I want thee, in everything, to glorify Me. Come, my child, and I will have a second transaction with thee, and if thou wilt come and transact with Me, as thou didst at conversion, and with a new meaning and a new depth and with new intensity of purpose, will yield thyself to Me, come and say, 'My God, I have begun to see what is wrong and how I have failed. I now want to come and give up everything to Thee; I want to give up self to Thee; I want to give up self confidence and self-effort.'" Then God will give answer, "My child, if thou art willing to go down into the death of Jesus, to come to the end of self, I will give the Holy Spirit fully in thee."

Jesus had to pass through the two stages. He was born the first time in Bethlehem, but He had to die. He had to give up the life of Bethlehem and He was born a second time out of the grave. He is called the firstborn from the dead[203]; he was born from the grave into a new life, a life of victory. His first life was a life without sin, but a life of weakness and very little power as compared with His life on the throne. And just so in your life, there can be these two stages. The first stage created in you a willing heart—brought you into the position of a child wishing to do God's will.

My child may wish to do my will, but he is unable to do it. He must grow up into a strong man. At 21 he comes of age, and then he can do it. God does not require 21 years to do His will, and He sometimes gives it to His child at conversion. But when the church is in such a feeble state as it now is, you find men living as Christians forty or fifty years without it.

I come, tonight, to plead with you and to say, God is willing, my brother, to lift you out of the lower to the higher stage, where you

---

[203] Colossians 1:18

can will and do, both. Don't you understand it is an absolute necessity? God must train us gradually, and God wants us to come to a right sense of our sinfulness and to a right sense of our utter helplessness. When He has so prepared us, He will make true, full Christians of us, with the Holy Spirit dwelling and ruling in us.

This brings me now to my fourth thought, and that is the question:

4. Wherein consists the secret of entering into this second blessing?

My answer is simply, entire dependence upon God. Let us now look at the text in Philippians, "Work out your own salvation, for it is God which worketh in you to will and to do."[204] Now just listen a moment. Which of these things must come first? "Work out your own salvation, for it is God that worketh in you." Which of the two must come first? Of course, God works in you. Work you, because God is working. Work you stands grammatically before God works but really and spiritually it comes after. Paul says, "God works, now you work." And oh friends, what is the great reason that you try to work and you cannot, that you will and cannot perform? Because you do not believe in the working of God. You try in your own strength to work. You take one half of the text, "Work out your own salvation," and you try hard, but you fail. Why? Because you do not take the first half—the foundation. Work you, because God is working in you, both to will and to do.

What God wants is to bring us there, where we let Him work. That is what we had yesterday about Christ bringing us to God. That is what we had this morning about our—when we are alive from the dead—at once coming and presenting ourselves unto God. Don't you begin to see that God must take a much larger and higher place in our life? If I want not only to will but also to do, then the Holy

---

[204] Philippians 2:12

Spirit must teach me to come and wait upon God with a dependence and with a helplessness and with a patience that I never exercised before. I must understand that every day of my life God must, directly from heaven, by the operation of His Holy Spirit, Himself do the working in me. Do you see that? Work for God worketh in you to will and to do.

Ah, it is no wonder that we *will* so much and *do* so little in the spiritual life, and that our life is so full of failure. God has not the place that God must have. It is not wrong that the whole heart of the sinner is occupied with Christ, for Christ wants to get hold of him and to win his love and to take him to Himself. But when once I am converted and in the hands of Christ, Christ wants to bring me on a step and to bring me to God that I may receive from God everything, just as Christ did Himself. Christ's whole life—we saw that yesterday morning—was dependence, dependence, dependence upon God and nothing else. Every morning and every night, from Bethlehem to Calvary, dependence upon God. And if Christ is living in me, and if my life is to be the life of Christ, and if my life is to be a life of power and of fruit and of work, I must let God work both to will and to do of His good pleasure.

Dear Christian friends, I ask myself sometimes, is not the reason of all the weakness in the church of Christ just this: people do not know their God? In the prophet Daniel we read that people who know their God shall be strong and do exploits. You must know your God! Your God is the great power in the universe that works everything. He keeps the sun shining. He keeps every little grass green. It is God that clothes the lilies with their beauty. How does He do it? Not from without—not from above, away at a distance— but He gives His life into the beautiful lily as it grows.

God is everywhere present in nature; and God wants to be much more distinctly and really, practically present in the heart of the believer. But we do not know it and we do not think about it. Why? It is because we do not listen to His word—"God worketh in you"—

and we do not let His Spirit teach us what God would do for us. Therefore, the question comes to us with unutterable solemnity: Does not the renewed will call us—call all of us—to a life of more dependence on God? Dear friends, if we will consent to live a life of nothingness, waiting upon the living God, He will work both to will and to do according to His good pleasure.

And now my last thought:

5. How to enter into this blessing

My first thought was: the renewed will proves the power of regeneration; it proves the impotence of the regenerate man and it proves the need of something new—a second blessing. And now the last thought: How are we to enter upon the blessing? Is there for us a prospect of real obedience? The man in Romans 7 had no real obedience. His heart was right, he was honest, but he failed. It was just the condition of the disciples before Pentecost. You know their hearts were right. Peter's heart was right when he said, "Lord, I will go to prison and to death with Thee."[205] He loved Jesus, he was honest, and that is why Christ did not reject him. He was honest but impotent—full of self-confidence and he deceived himself. There was the will, but he could not perform.

Look at Gethsemane. Christ said of His disciples when He found them sleeping, "The spirit is willing, but the flesh is weak."[206] A word of the deepest spiritual significance. "My beloved disciples, there is in you a spirit that is willing. You love Me and want to watch with Me, but the flesh is too strong and you can't do it. The power of the Spirit has not yet conquered the power of the flesh." But when the Holy Ghost came at Pentecost, the power of the Spirit conquered the flesh and they were able to do anything, even

---

[205] Luke 22:33
[206] Matthew 26:41

though they had to suffer for Jesus.

Dear friends, how can we enter into this blessing? There is one step. One thing is needful.[207] And what is that? Giving up our life to God. Can we do it tonight? Yes, we can, if the heart is prepared.

Just think now for a moment back and ask yourself, "Has the picture of Romans 7 been your photograph"? Have you not had to say, "That is exactly my condition"? Give answer. When the man cries here, "To will is present with me, but how to perform I know not,"[208] has not that been true of your life very largely? Come, say so if it is before God. And say, "Alas! alas! Too much that has been my life." Well, do you want to remain in that condition? Or would you love to come to a life in which God will work in you both to will and to do so that when God makes you will anything that is good, you may be certain that God will help you carry it out? God will work to do in you all things good. Do you long for that? Would not you long, beloved Christians, to do the blessed will of God? "Blessed are they that hear the word of God and do it."[209] Oh, the blessedness of knowing that I do the will of God! Do you not long for that blessed life? Well, now you have heard about the impotence of the regenerate man. Don't try any longer to flog and spur and urge yourself with the thought, "You must try more, you must do better, you must pray more." It will not help you in this matter. You must come to despair of your present condition. "Here am I, a child of God, knowing and loving God's will, wanting to do it, longing to do it, and yet failing. Is there no help for me?"

Thank God, there is help! And here is the help—Philippians 2:13: "It is God which worketh in you both to will and to do." "Work out your own salvation with fear and trembling," for God will work in you. And isn't that the one step I am tonight to take? Out of the life

---

[207] Luke 10:42
[208] Romans 7:18
[209] Luke 11:28

of failure and the life of wrongdoing and the life of Romans 7 so that I cry, "O wretched man that I am, who shall deliver?"[210] and that I cry, "I thank God, through Jesus Christ there is deliverance?"[211] Is that not the step? And then as I say, "I thank God," that I come and present myself to God again as we had it this morning—as alive from the dead—and I say, "Lord God, now I begin to understand it. As alive from the dead I must present myself to Thee every day and every hour, for the power must come from Thee alone. When Thou hadst placed the will in me and the delight in the law of my God, I thought that that was all and that now I must try and carry it out. How I have failed! Now I come and present myself unto God—unto God Himself"?

We heard this morning why. We heard this morning how—in thanksgiving, in entire surrender to be entirely His, but above all in holy expectancy—we are to say to God, "This life was begun by Thee and must be continued by Thee every minute." A tree can only live on the root from which it springs. If an oak springs today from an acorn, the oak can stand a hundred years; but it must always stand in the root from which it springs up to-day. And so if your new life has sprung up from God, it can only root in God every day; and unless there is contact with God every moment, and unless there is the filling from God every moment to work the do in you, your life must be feeble.

Oh come, Christian, and say, "Though God regenerated me, and gave me a new heart and a new will, that is not enough. God must give me—and He will give me—the power to carry out the new will." God will do it.

Oh come, let us surrender ourselves to God this very night and enter into a covenant with Him. Dear friends, let us come. Let us plead for pardon, let us surrender ourselves and trust for mercy. I

---

[210] Romans 7:24
[211] Romans 7:25

do not know if all are prepared for it. I do not know if the majority are prepared for it. But if there were only ten souls here tonight who have begun to say, "I see there is a second blessing, I see there is a life of liberty and victory, I see there is a life, not only of willing but of actual performance, I see there is a life of power in which the Holy Ghost comes and enables a man to do God's will—I want that life!" Let them say, "Lord, accept of me. Lord, fulfill now in me, Thy word. I believe Thou wilt henceforth work in me to will and to do."

Amen.

15. Jesus Able to Keep
(2 Timothy 1:12)

In the second Epistle to Timothy, the first chapter and the 12th verse, you have these words:

> *"I know whom I have believed and am persuaded that He is able to keep that which I have committed unto Him against that day."*

I chose that text under the impression that for many this would be our last gathering, as all cannot come tomorrow morning. And I thought that if in any heart a desire had been stirred during our meetings to enter the blessed life, that this word might help them tonight, for it will lead us up to a simple act of committal and consecration. But this morning I got a request from some 12 or 15 brethren in the ministry, or in the work of God, asking me to give a testimony as to my own personal experience in the Christian life. And before I speak of these words I want, in a few short sentences, to tell you how God has led me.

What God has done to me is not mine but His own, and if it can help you, I cannot withhold it. And yet I am somewhat reluctant to speak of my experience for this reason: when a man has got a clear, distinct experience to tell and a very definite story about something God has done for him—a clear passing out of one state of the Christian life into another—it is often very helpful and very stirring. But that is not my story. I was away in South Africa, almost alone and I had to fight and stumble my way along, and owing to that I had no such clear path as I could have wished for; but let me tell you.

If I speak of my life, my Christian life—the first fifteen years perhaps, I call a time of darkness and of struggling after the light. I could divide my Christian life into three periods: The time of darkness, the time of the vision of the light, and then the time of the richer experience. I was, as a young minister, most earnest. I was counted a most faithful gospel preacher, and I was diligent in the enormous parish that was entrusted to me. I loved my work and yet all the time my spiritual life was one of deep unhappiness. I was bound in the chains of misapprehension and prejudice.

One thing that I thought was that a Christian must go on sinning every day. I really thought that this was a must. As a result of that, I had no definite expectation that God would keep me from it. I am sorry to say that that was my belief, and then along with that I had no conception that obedience was a possible thing. I look back with shame when, in later years, I began to see the place that obedience ought to take in a Christian life. I remember how little I understood that—that Christianity is to give up your self to entire obedience to God. I never saw it. And then, along with that, I had no real faith in the keeping, sanctifying power of God's Holy Spirit or of Jesus Christ. Yet I was most earnest, studying the matter of sanctification, praying about it, but I got very little light. But it was a time on which God looked with mercy, for it was a time of great desire and often of crying to God, and God hears cries.

Let me say, for the help of anyone who is in that state of desire, that there was a little story that helped me wonderfully at that time. There is a book in English, 'Parables from Nature' by Mrs Gatty.[212] One of these parables is this:

She represents a number of crickets meeting and talking together. You know there are different sorts of crickets—the field cricket and the grass cricket and the tree cricket and so on. The crickets were comparing notes and one said, "Oh, I had to seek a long time till I found a house, but afterwards I got into the bark of an old tree

---

[212] Margaret Gatty (1809–1973)

where there was a hole, and I felt that was just exactly my place and, oh, I am so happy there." That was the tree cricket. And another said, "Well, you know I once came to you, and I couldn't get comfortable there. But afterwards I found my right place. I climbed up on the high grass and I clung there, and I wave backwards and forwards as the wind swings the grass, and oh, I feel so happy there. That is just my place." That was the grass cricket. And another cricket began to tell where it stayed and found itself happy. And at last there was one cricket said, "Alas, I have tried all these places, but I can't get comfortable. There is something in me always cold and there is no place for me." Then a wise old mother cricket, that was present, said, "My child, don't say that. You are speaking against your Creator. Depend upon it—if God created you, He has got a place waiting for you, and you will find it out." So they parted. Sometime after they met again and were again telling their experiences; then this cricket began to tell its story and to say, "Yes, I have found my place at last. You know since that time men have come to this island, and as soon as they had built a house I crept in; they had made a fire and I found that is just the place for me, and I got into a corner of the hearth and I am so comfortable and happy there. I am sure that is my place." That was the hearth cricket.

And then the application that the book made was this: that when God has created a need, He will fulfil it.

Oh, if there are any hungry and thirsty souls, walking in darkness and struggling along and saying they cannot understand it, or trying to understand it and complaining that they can't reach it, I say to them, lift up your hearts to God in trust. The God that created your heart for Himself, and the God that made you His child in Christ, He will provide for your holiness if you will trust Him more. Look away from all teaching. Use it as a help when you can but look away from it to the living God. He made you and He can make you holy.

Well, as I said, I suppose for fifteen years after my conversion I went on, and then came the time when in England there was a great stir about the higher life and I got some of these books and they helped me wonderfully, and I then began to say, "Yes, there is a better life." It was at that time, now thirty years ago, in a time of revival in my Dutch parish in Worcester, South Africa, that I wrote "Abide in Christ" in Dutch. It was not perhaps exactly the same as now, but the substance. It was at that time that my heart was feeling after the truth and beginning to find it, beginning to get hold of something, a little of the blessed experience of better knowledge of God and of more trust in Him. And yet I have to confess with shame that at that time I often stumbled. One thing was, I had never been taught the absolute necessity, the supreme importance of literal, immediate, actual obedience to God. Someone said to me about that book, "I think you have put it more from the privilege side than from the duty side." Perhaps that is true. I had not at that time sufficiently seen the call to absolute obedience.

So it went on, year after year. I enjoyed more of God, I enjoyed more rest, I enjoyed more peace, I got more victory, and I learned to trust God more. The path God led me in was not that of one decisive crisis, but step by step. Mind, I have great faith that God is willing to take a man in by a sudden step by a crisis in his life and I count it a very blessed thing, and I think the reason that God did not take me in that way was simply that I was not properly instructed. I had no Christian friends of experience around me to help, and when you haven't any help in that way, you often fail on some little point of obedience or faith and then you fall back again. But then God led me on, in His great mercy, I at times failing, yet at times in great peace, till later on—it would be difficult to say, exactly how long, for there was no actual transition—I can see that when I contrast the last fifteen years of my life with the first fifteen, I praise God for a very great difference. And what I praise God for is this: the rest of faith. I can see that He has taught me to rest in Him and to trust Him, and to believe even if my faith does not always rise to its fullest height, but yet to continue in the abiding belief that my God is working in me; that my God loves me with a wonderful love, and that as I yield entirely to Him He will do a perfect work in me. Oh friends, that is what we need, tonight, those who haven't it. To come into that rest—that rest with God which leaves everything with Him.

And what God has done more for me is this: He has helped me, I trust, to greater and more continued obedience. I do not say it is perfect, but by the grace of God I have learned to do His will, and to do it as a thing unto Himself personally, and I have found the peace and blessing of it. One thing more. It has pleased God to use my labors for the helping of His children out in the land where I live and elsewhere, and I cannot sufficiently praise His goodness that it has pleased Him to use me as a vessel—an earthen, empty, broken vessel into which He has poured out His life and of His love and of the living water to bring to others. There is my simple, short testimony. There was a time, a third of my Christian life, that was in great darkness; there was perhaps another third seeking God and the light and rejoicing in it and yet not getting full access; another third in which God has brought me out deeper into the enjoyment of His life and His love. Praised be His holy name!

And now with these few words, I got courage to say them because I find that Paul here gives a personal testimony. And what Paul testifies is this: he says, "I commit everything to God." Oh, there have been times in my life when I have understood what that was and experienced it on the strength of that word. He committed himself to Christ and then he looked up and he saw Christ, able in His mighty power to keep him, and he said, "Praise God for an Almighty Christ." And then when he had committed himself, he trusted Christ to accept him, and he trusted Christ also to keep him. That is what he says here, "I know Him, in whom I have believed, and I am persuaded, I am confident, that He is able to keep, and that He does keep that which I have committed unto Him unto that day."[213]

Dear friends, I feel it is an unutterably solemn thing to have this last meeting this evening. I feel very deeply what an awfully solemn thing it is to speak to God's people about a life of holiness and not really help them up into it. I feel very deeply how little I am able to speak aright about the sin and the low state of God's people. I feel how little I am able to show them what the unbelief and the want of righteousness and the fruitlessness of that mixed life which so many live. I feel what a solemn thing it is that I am not able to sound the trumpet as I ought to and to awaken them out of sleep and to call them and to make them feel, "Man, you can't live one day longer in this low carnal life, you must come out undividedly for Christ." Oh, that I could sound the trumpet. I feel above all how helpless I am to speak tonight what I thought to speak about the Lord Jesus Christ. He is ready, in His almighty love and power, to take hold of every child of God in this house—however far back or low down he is—if he will give himself into His almighty keeping. May God Himself exalt His blessed Son in the midst of us to-night.

I want to speak about three points:

1. What it is to commit ourselves to Christ

2. What it is to know Him as an almighty keeper

3. What it is to be assured that He will keep us

Shall we not, before we speak further, unite in quiet prayer to God for His Holy Spirit.

(Prayer)

You know the words of the text, "I know Him, whom I have believed, and I am persuaded that He is able to keep that which I

---

[213] 2 Timothy 1:12

have committed unto Him against that day." I said, three points.
First, look at this entire committal of everything to Christ; second,
look at Christ as the mighty keeper; and third, look at Paul with his
confident persuasion, "Christ will keep me."

1. What it is to commit ourselves to Christ

In the first place, the committal. What does that mean? People
have sometimes asked, "What was it that Paul committed to
Christ?" Some have said it was his life, in the midst of so much
persecution and danger; others have said it was his ministry, the
work that he had to do, as an apostle; others have said it was his
own soul, with his spiritual life and his hope of the crown of
righteousness. I think it is impossible to separate these things. I
think Paul meant them all, for he had committed himself wholly to
Christ Jesus. And now what does that word "commit" mean? In the
Greek it is the very word that is used for what we call in our
commercial business in banks, a deposit.

You all know what the deposit is in a bank. I have a thousand
dollars to spare and I don't know what to do with it; if I keep it, it
may get stolen, or I may be tempted to use it too soon, or it lies
there without interest. I go to the bank and I give that thousand
dollars to the bank and I say, "Now take care of it for me." And the
bank gives me what they call in England—I suppose it is the same
in America—a deposit receipt. And so Paul says, "I made a deposit
of myself with the Lord Jesus." And you know that that deposit of
the thousand dollars in the bank is mine, but the bank keeps it for
me and the bank uses it for me and they pay me so much interest.
The bank asks me when I go to deposit it, "For how long will you
deposit it?" Suppose I deposit it there for five years. I leave it there
and I get the interest regularly. They keep it; it is mine, but it is in
their hands.

Now, that is exactly what Paul did. He said, "I cannot keep myself.
I have got a very precious thing. I have got a heart and a life and a

wonderful soul created by God, but I cannot keep it. Sin and the world and the flesh and the devil are all tempting me and wanting to rob me of my powers; what shall I do? I will give it up to Christ to keep." And he did. He gave himself wholly—his head, his heart, his mind, his affections, his will, his powers, his body, his righteousness that he had formerly, his property, his religion—everything he gave up to Christ and said, "Lord, do with it as seemeth good in Thy sight and keep it for me." That, dear friends, is simply and exactly what a man has got to do if he wants to enter into the higher life.

The great mischief with Christians is that they have given over their souls to Jesus to keep and say, "Lord, keep my soul and let me never perish." That is what many people pray. But they have said, "Lord, let me keep my will; let me keep my own mind and read and think what I like; let me keep my position and let me keep my own money." They ask to keep a great many things and they never, never, can have peace or rest. The Lord Jesus comes and says he wants all, all, *all*.

And that is the solemn question with which I come to every Christian tonight. Brother, have you given up everything you have into the keeping of Jesus? Or do you not often talk just what you like? About this and that man you say exactly what you choose, sharp or foolish things, just as you like. You haven't given up your tongue to Jesus. Your thoughts. Do you not often spend your thoughts upon yourself or upon the world, just as you like? You have never yet said to the Redeemer, "My mind, with every power, belongs to the Holy Christ who bought me with His blood." I want you to come tonight, if you have never said so, and say, "Christ shall have all."

I want to go deeper. I want to say, are there sins of which you never have said, "I give that up to Christ"? There is the love of the world. Are you going to say tonight, "I am going to part with the world and to give this heart, this life of mine to love Christ—to love Christ

only, to love Christ with the love that the Holy Spirit has given me."
Dear friends, you all want the higher life, the life of faith, and the
life of Christ, but remember, we must pay the price. We must get
rid of everything, and Christ Jesus must have us all in all.

May God, by His Holy Spirit, work conviction in the hearts of His
children while I ask the question solemnly: "Christian, what are
you here for, tonight?" Can you say, "I know of nothing in my life
that I have not really put into the hands of Jesus and that He has
not got and that He is not keeping for me?" Can you say that? If
you cannot say it, ask what is the hindrance. There may be more
than one hindrance, but the first and chief hindrance will be this:
that you are not absolutely willing to part with it.

I fear we do not understand how literally and how absolutely the
Holy God in Christ wants to have us for Himself. I cannot fill a
vessel unless the vessel is absolutely empty and at my disposal, and
God cannot fill us with Himself and the divine life unless we get
utterly empty of everything, and unless we come and give ourselves
entirely and unreservedly into His hands. Now come tonight. Are
you willing? But remember, there can be no success if you keep
back anything.

You have, perhaps, heard the story of a rich lady, in England. She
had a splendid box of jewelry—diamonds and rings and pearls. She
was going to travel on the continent and she came to a friend and
she said, "This is a very valuable box of jewelry and I am afraid of
leaving it in the house when I am away, in case it might be stolen;
so I come and ask you to take charge of it." And the lady said, "Very
good." There were thirty or forty articles in the box; she took out
five of them in the presence of her friend to be used when
traveling. The box was locked and handed to the friend. The lady
went on her travels and after a couple of months she came to her
friend and she asked for her box of jewelry. And the friend said,
"There it is, but where are the things you took with you?" Her
answer was: "I am sorry to say that they got stolen, I have lost

them." You see that all she entrusted to the friend was safe, and all that she took charge of herself was lost.

This is just the way with us. All that you try to keep in your own hands and manage gets lost. Try and keep your own tongue—take charge of your tongue and keep that; you will fail and you will sin. Try and keep charge of your temper; you will fail and you will sin. All you try to keep charge of yourself you lose, but come and bring everything into the keeping of Jesus and you can depend upon it you will never repent.

Are you willing to come, tonight, and to say, "Lord Jesus, I want to be a man utterly given up to God, so that everybody can see it. I want to be a man with nothing for myself, walking just in the deepest humility and dependence, and letting God glorify Himself in me. I want to be a man sacrificing everything for the sake of God's Son and God's love. I want to be a man wholly and unreservedly given to God, that God may do His very best with me." Is that your desire? Then I invite you to come, however feeble and however unworthy. Christ is waiting. You never can honor and glorify God in the way you are living now, but come and commit yourself to the keeping of Jesus, and will He not prove faithful? Will He not gloriously and wondrously keep you and bless you?

2. What it is to know Christ as an almighty keeper

And now, secondly: look at the mighty keeper. Paul said, "I am persuaded that He is able to keep."[214] Oh, the mighty keeping of Jesus! May God open our eyes to see that.

Dear friends, there was a time, when I was a young minister—I remember it very well—that when I read of the omnipotence of God that I thought, "Well that is not one of the principal attributes

[214] 2 Timothy 1:12

of God that I have to do with." We make a difference in theology between the natural attributes of God and the moral attributes. The moral attributes are holiness, goodness, righteousness, truth and faithfulness. They have to do with character, and I thought that that is what a Christian has to do with. But the natural attributes that can be seen in creation, wisdom, omnipotence and such like, I thought of minor importance. After a time, I began to find out how wrong I was, for I began to find out in reading the Bible that at the bottom of all faith is omnipotence, the mighty power of God.

I read about Abraha, how God met him and said, "I am God Almighty,"[215] and I saw that thought was the rock upon which Abraham stood. I found so often in the history of Israel, that God came and appealed to His own mighty power in His promises; I came down to the New Testament and I found how Jesus said that "the things that are impossible with men are possible with God,"[216] and I began to see that one of the attributes that I need most in my spiritual life is the omnipotence of God; and I need nothing less than that to trust in. And I think I am learning every day more that that is what I need to rest in, because the whole work that is to be done in me—in keeping, sanctifying and teaching me—is all a work of God's omnipotence.

And then, dear friends, there is the Lord Jesus Christ. I used to preach upon His miracles with great pleasure, and I always spoke of His mighty power; but it was only later on that I began to see that that that almighty power must not only be exercised when a man is pardoned and made a child of God, but that almighty power must be exercised every moment in my life. Every moment. There is not five minutes in the day that I do not need the almighty keeper to keep charge of me. And when a man sees that, and he reads the miracles in the gospels, he ever says, "Praise God, that is my Lord Jesus." Whether I see Him healing the sick, or feeding the

---

[215] Genesis 17:1
[216] Luke 18:27

hungry, or raising the dead, or calming the storm, I can say, "That is my Christ, in whose keeping my soul is."

Beloved, have you learned to understand that? I need an almighty keeper to keep me right. Oh friends, you talk about having your temper kept, or your tongue kept, or your wandering heart kept, or your patience kept; what is the reason you have failed when you have entrusted these to Jesus? One reason is this: your unbelief. You have not gone and said, "Now the Almighty God—here in Chicago, in a place of business, where I am tempted to forget God, where I am tempted to be ashamed of Him—here in Chicago, the almighty power of God is with me in Christ to keep me all the day long."

Oh, that I could get souls tonight to trust the almightiness of God for their daily life! You need it, my brother, my sister, for your daily life! You do not need it now and then on great occasions, but you need it for every hour of your life—the Almighty Christ to keep you right every day. Will you not come tonight and worship this Almighty Christ, of whom Paul tells, "I believe and am persuaded that He is able to keep what I commit unto Him!"

3. What it is to be assured that He will keep us

Then comes my third thought: the faith in this almighty keeper. Yes, that is the most blessed part of it. Paul says, "I know Him whom I have believed and that is why I am persuaded that He is able to keep and that He will keep and that He does keep what I have committed to Him." If we were to ask Paul, if we could ask Him and say, "Paul, what do you mean when you say, 'I know Him whom I have believed,' how do you know Him?" He would answer, "He loved me and gave Himself for me. I found that out. He came to me when I was His enemy and He conquered me and He blessed me, and He poured His Spirit and His life into me, and He revealed His love, and I learned to know Him, the Lamb of God who had purchased me with His blood; I know whom I have believed—the crucified Jesus—and I cannot doubt Him ever again." And he would say further—for he was an old man when he wrote this epistle—he would say, "I have known Him for twenty years, and year by year and time after time, in trial and trouble and persecution and deep suffering and sorrow, in times of apparently utter helplessness I have tried Him and I have always found Him a faithful friend and a loving Master and a blessed Companion and an Almighty God to help me. I know whom I have believed."

You have your testimony meetings here on earth often, and I often love to be at a testimony meeting. It has done my heart good many a time. I call up Paul tonight and I say, "Paul, I want you to speak so this company of believers tonight, and I want to invite and encourage every one of them to give up all to Christ. Paul, what do you say to that?" And Paul would say, "He is worthy of it, a thousand times over. Worthy is the Lamb that was slain." And he would say, "Christians, do not stand back; come and do it." If any Christian trembles and says, "Paul, I am so feeble and so unworthy and so unfaithful. Paul, what have you to say to me?" He would say, "I know in whom I have believed. He is the loving One. I was the chief of sinners, a transgressor and blasphemer, and He had mercy upon me, that in me He might show forth the glory of His grace." And Paul would say, "I know Him whom I have believed. His love passeth knowledge, His power is without limit," and He would say, "Souls, trust Christ tonight."

Are you going to do it? Are you going to say it? I hear that man speak, "I know whom I have believed." Remember, it was a matter of faith. Paul had times of trial and of darkness and of humiliation and of suffering—indescribable—and nothing could have held him up but trust in God. He says once he had the sentence of death in himself that he should not learn to trust in himself but in the living God alone—in God who raised the dead, the Almighty God, and so he says of Christ, "I know in whom I have believed, and I have put my trust in Him, and I have never been put to shame and therefore I am persuaded He will keep, He is able to keep, and He will do it unto that day." Paul knew that there was a crown of righteousness laid up for him with positive certainty and he said, "He will keep what I have committed unto Him, unto that great day."

And now, dear friends, now we want to come to the application. You know what we have got to do tonight. We want to take three simple steps.

i. The first step is this: I want to invite you to commit yourself absolutely, unreservedly to the Lord Jesus and to His almighty keeping. I want that to be a transaction here tonight. A transaction. And therefore, I prayed and I pray again, "Oh Christ, be Thou so present here that every soul that is willing may feel that nearness, and take courage and put itself into Thy hands."

Come, beloved, with all your feebleness, with all your sins and shortcomings and backslidings; come with all the darkness that at this very hour may still be in your soul; come, beloved, with all the difficulties that are before you. You have said, "If you knew my circumstances you would not think it was so easy to live the blessed life." I tell you I know that there are circumstances of tremendous difficulty, but Jesus Christ is almighty! Oh come, will you not tonight come and commit yourself to Him?

ii. And then the second step: When you commit yourself, the second step is to believe, "Now the Lord Jesus does take me just for what I commit myself to Him. I committed myself to Him formerly for conversion and He accepted me; I commit myself to be kept— He accepts me." "I have committed myself more than once," someone will say, "for a new blessing and I got a new blessing, but it didn't last. But I want to commit myself tonight to an everlasting keeper to be kept every day, every hour, in the power of the Holy Spirit." This is, indeed, a solemn thing to say, but God is willing in one moment to give it to an honest soul, and therefore I give my message with great confidence and joy. Christ is willing to accept you tonight and to take you into His keeping. Will you not now come and trust Him and say, "Jesus, I believe that Thou art here present, and take charge of me."

iii. And then comes the third step. That is to say, "Now I am persuaded that He will keep me." Before I leave the house tonight, I look at the difficulties that I may have to meet tomorrow and next day, and what difficulties I carry about in my own heart or temperament, and I say, "Jesus, canst Thou keep me all along the line—through this week, up to the end of the year, of next year, '96[217], if I live?" Can Jesus keep me day by day? Paul says He can; the whole of God's word says He can; there are believers who can testify He can. Will you not tonight say, "He can, I am sure He can"? He will do it for anyone who will give himself up to Him and entrust himself to Him.

Oh come, young people, with your precious, beautiful young lives to live of twenty or thirty or forty years before you, what a beautiful thing to begin life better than I did, better than others have done—to begin life young and fresh for eternity and say, "Every breath, every pulse, shall be for Jesus." Come tonight. Come, you who are farther on in the path of life, you men in the midst of business, you women in the cares of the daily life. Come, oh come tonight.

Let us all come to our God in Christ. Come and look at your life; then gaze at Christ and His keeping, and come and trust Him tonight to do it. Old men and old women, I call upon every Christian, and if there are unconverted people here who have never done it, they can come with us, and they can begin tonight and say, "Christ, Thou wouldst have me holy; if Thou wilt make me holy, and if Thou wilt keep me day by day, tonight I will give up my soul into the hands of my Creator."

Come tonight! You know how there have been times of war when a town was in danger of being attacked that people would bring to

---

[217] These lectures were given in 1895, so the next year was 1896

the bank their valuables to be taken care of. It would be said, "Let all who are afraid bring their gold and silver plate or anything that they have and have it locked up in the bank." People came and the doors were set open and everyone brought his treasures and got them safely locked in case their houses outside might be burned down or broken open. And, oh friends, I say tonight: Christ, the great manager of the heavenly bank, of the heavenly place of refuge, the great keeper of the treasures of God, flings the door wide open. His arms are outstretched and His heart is open and He is looking out to see who will commit himself to His keeping.

Who will give Him what His heart longs for? Who will come tonight and trust all that is precious in life to his Almighty Lord? Who will come tonight and give up His whole life into the keeping of Jesus, in the confidence that He will keep it safe? Come, let us do it now.

Let us bow our heads in prayer.

16. The Life of Rest
(Philippians 4:5-6)

Now this morning I want to take one of the very simplest thoughts of God's word as the subject of my address. We have been speaking for two weeks about the spiritual life, but you know where the spiritual life is to be put into practice: in the everyday life. And today, therefore, I want to come down very low, to the level of our everyday Christianity. It is in the rush of daily life that the presence of God is to be experienced, and His power to be proved.

We began last week by speaking about the work of the Holy Spirit. I tried to point out to you what God intends that Spirit to be in your daily life, in your walk as holy and spiritually minded men, in a walk in love and humility. I tried to point what the great hindrances are to a spiritual life, especially self. I tried to point out what the blessedness is that will come if we give ourselves to the leading of the Spirit, and what the object is for which we are to seek it. Then we came this week to speak about the work of Christ. I began by pointing out that His great work is just to bring us very near to God, and how I believe that this is a great want in the church of Christ. We need more of God, more humble waiting upon God in our private prayer and worship, and in public services.

God must take the first place in everything; we must take time to wait upon God for God to take that place in our souls. I then spoke about how Christ came to exhibit just this one thing: a life of absolute dependence upon God. He came to reveal to us that God was everything to Him. We spoke of other parts of His work, and last night we closed by speaking about Jesus Christ in His blessed work as an Almighty Keeper, and ended by a consecration meeting in which we gave up ourselves to Him; God grant that many souls may know what it is that the Everlasting God is keeping them.

And now we have to go away to our daily life—our homes, our business, our studies, our duties—and all of you know by experience that it is just there that the failure comes in. It is all right in my closet and it is all right in my worship and all right in my work when I am speaking for Christ, but oh, the times of relaxation, the times when I am off my guard, and times when I am in the duties of this life—these are the times when failures come; and the great question now arises, "How can I live so that not only on the mount of worship, but down low in the valley of the most ordinary everyday life I may have unbroken the sense of the presence of God?"

Dear friends, if you want the revelation of God, I have told you more than once you must take more time in prayer and have daily fellowship with God. You must take more time in your secret hour of prayer just quietly to realize God and adore Him. But the fullest revelation of God cannot satisfy unless it is carried out in the daily life. The value of contact with God every day, and the value of the power of the Holy Ghost daily, and the value of Christ as a keeper must be proved in daily life. More than one begins to ask, "Will it last, the blessing I have got? Will I be faithful? Will it ever be carried out in my daily life?"

Listen to the word I have for you this morning. It is one of the simplest descriptions of the life of faith. Philippians 4:5-6:

> "Be careful [or anxious] for nothing, but in everything by prayer and supplication with thanksgiving let your requests be made known unto God."

Here we have a restful life. It is the life of continual trust, continual prayer, continual praise, continual peace, continual safety. Five blessed marks of the blessed life.

1. Continual trust

The restful life is a life of continual trust. That is where it begins. You notice that we have the name of God in these two verses twice. In the first verse it is, "bring your needs, your requests, unto God"—that is to say, let God be the one object of your trust; and then comes in the second verse, and God will be a fountain of blessing to you: "The peace of God will keep you." These are the two sides. My love must be turned to God and God's love and blessing will be turned to me.

"Be anxious for nothing." You know how difficult it is to obey that command. You hear people tell, when you talk about the higher life, "Oh, if you only knew my circumstances." At Northfield[218] a man told me, "It is all very well at a convention, but one does come into such difficulties in business that it is almost impossible to expect that you will always be kept in perfect peace." Now here comes the word of God, dear children of God who gave yourselves up last night. Learn the lesson, "Be anxious for nothing." And why? Because you have a God that cares for you.

Oh, I wish I could say to my friends and myself what I see sometimes! Is God going to do everything so perfectly in nature all around me, and is the only place He is going to fail here in my life? Look at the sun. For thousands of years how perfectly it has been shining, with what abiding fruitfulness it has blessed the earth. So perfect it cannot be more perfect, and it was God that made it shine. Look on the earth, at these trees and flowers and the green grass. Look at the bird, the animal, or fish—each one so perfectly fitted to show forth the glory, wisdom and power of God. And is God not able to work as perfectly in the heart of His child? And is the only place of failure to be your heart and mine? I cannot believe it.

I believe that the God who works so gloriously in the universe is willing to work more gloriously in your heart, so that your heart

---

[218] An annual convention organised by D.L. Moody

shall be the scene where His glory is fully revealed—the manifestation of what God's love and power can do. But why does He not do it? Because you won't let Him. Because you don't trust Him. Because you allow circumstances to come between you and God. Because you in your heart believe circumstances are stronger than God. You think, "God cannot deliver me from their power." You have not got fully under the power of the promises and love of God. This word comes, "Be anxious for nothing." God is willing to take charge of everything. Apply that to external things. One may be in adversity, another may be surrounded by enemies, another may not be able to keep his engagements. There comes the word, "Be anxious for nothing."

You know how depressing it is to have unconverted relatives. Are you not to be anxious about that? No. "Be anxious for nothing." How can that be? In this way alone—that I carry all the care and the trouble and the circumstances to the living God, and that I wait upon Him until I get sight of my God undertaking and taking complete charge. When my soul gets sight of that the anxiety goes away and I rest in the perfect trust—God cares, God has charge, and God will guide me right. Apply that to your spiritual life.

I know there are those here who are in great difficulty about their spiritual life. They have taken the step last night, but they have done it more than once before. There is a note of fear in their hearts: "Will it last? I have such a temper, I have such a disposition, I have such little help in those around me. There are a thousand things around me to draw me back." I come to point you to what Jesus Christ did: He came to bring us to God. If as His humble, feeble servant I can take you and lead you to your God, my work will be done.

What is a God for? A God is meant to be the light and life of all nature and existence. A God lives for this. We need a God to be the only power that works throughout the universe. A God is meant to have charge of the creatures He has made and to fill their life with

His blessedness. Look at your God! Never did a mother care for a little child with such watchful tenderness from morning to night as your God is willing to take charge of your spiritual and your external life. Do you know this God? Have you learned to say, "I do trust Thee. I have no anxiety, for my God provides. He is God Almighty and His promises are so wonderful and He is so loving and tender. I will trust my God."

Who is going to say, this morning, "God help me. I want to have not a single anxiety. I am going to trust God"? God will do His work beautifully and blessedly, and most gloriously. Children of God, "Be careful for nothing."

You know the sixth chapter of Matthew with those precious words of the Lord Jesus.[219] They are not only for poor people who have no clothes, but they are meant for every one of us. If God clothe the lilies with His beauty how much more will He clothe you? Just think of that. How does God clothe the lilies? Not from without. He puts within the life that grows up into them and with most beautiful freshness there comes up a lily. A lily has the life of God—the Spirit of nature that comes from God working in it. God clothed that lily, and will God not much more clothe you and me with the beauty of holiness and of humility. Oh Christian, take this word, "Be careful for nothing." The restful life is a life of continual trust.

2. Continual prayer

The next mark of a restful life. "In everything by prayer and supplication let your requests be known unto God." Continual prayer. It is in prayer that you will learn the secret of trusting. If you take but little time to pray, you will have but little power to trust. Trust toward God is not natural to us. Trust is very natural to us to ward a fellow man. When a man tells me a thing, I do not take

---

[219] Matthew 6:25-34

a moment to believe. We are on the platform of nature. When my God speaks, we are on another platform. God is the Invisible One, a Spirit of holiness, and I can trust Him only by the Holy Spirit coming into me. If I live under the leading of the Holy Spirit, my heart grows larger, my capacity of trust is increased, my eyes are opened up, and I see the glory and limitless promises of God and the treasures of His grace. I see His heart and Omnipotent love actually engaged in blessing me, and my heart learns to rejoice in Him. In prayer I learn to trust Him.

Remember this, "In everything." That means temporal things, that means spiritual things, that means great things and that means little things. Some people pray about the great things, great troubles, but not about the little things. That is wrong in the life of faith. Some think that the word means, "All I can manage I keep in my own hands, and all I cannot manage I may expect God to take care of." This is not the way. God must have all committed to Him. One asks me, "How can I know the will of God in a difficulty?" My brother, the way to know that in difficulty is to follow the will of God in simple things. Let the Holy Spirit show you the will of God in little things every day, and when great perplexities come, the Holy Spirit will reveal God's will.

What a privilege it is amid the worries of daily life and difficult circumstances to leave them all with God. Just to say, "Lord, these circumstances I bring them all to Thee, I entrust them to Thee." By prayer and supplication I can put them into my Father's bosom indefinitely. I can give them over to Him and I can rest there until conscious that the Spirit assures me they are in God's hands. In more prayer you will learn the secret of trust in spiritual things. How often we go to a minister, or to a teacher, or books (not that I am depreciating teachers or books, but when we depend upon them, they come between us and God). How often we have questions and say, "I wish I could ask that question. I wish he would tell us what he thinks," instead of going with every question to God and saying, "I do not expect the voice of an angel to bring an answer at once, but I want in answer to prayer to put the difficulty in the bosom of the Father, and I know by the secret inworking of the Holy Spirit He will give me light on it and lead in a right path." Let your life be full of prayer.

I have spoken about this need of daily fellowship with God. I have put a few thoughts together and had them put in print to be distributed among the friends. They contain some instructions as to how the soul ought to cultivate daily fellowship with God—in taking the place before God, in realizing His presence, in taking our place in Christ Jesus in deepest humility, and counting upon the work of the Holy Spirit. If you will follow these instructions, or any others in God's word, you will find it such a blessed thing to come and bow before God and present your petitions. But you say, "Is God not listening to what I say before I have felt the consciousness." Such prayer helps very little. "By prayer and supplication make your requests known unto God." Let your heart feel that you have made it known to God. God will answer, "I have heard; leave it with me." If you will thus pray your prayers, there will be a new joy, a very fountain of blessing opened up to you. May God make us all men of prayer.

Remember that the apostle says, "In everything." It does not mean only about your own needs, but the blessedness of prayer is, it gives me power with God as intercessor. The great work of my Lord Jesus is to be always interceding. There is no more heavenly work than intercession. And yet how much neglected, how little practiced! Let us learn by prayer and supplication to bring everything that might make us anxious to God. Here is a minister with a congregation—how many things he has to make him anxious! His own weakness, his own spiritual life, the state of his members, some worldly Christians, some unconverted people—how much to make him anxious! What a privilege in intercession to get rid of it all, and throw it into the bosom of Jehovah, and to say, "I have made it known to God. That is enough."

There is a great deal in the church and its worldliness that might well make us tremendously anxious. Some are deceiving themselves with a great deal of formality, with a great deal of head-knowledge, and the real personal love of Jesus is wanting. But oh, do not let us bear our burdens and anxieties ourselves, but learn the rest of trust, the rest of faith. The blessed life is the life of continual prayer, pouring into the heart of God everything that comes into my heart.

3. Continual praise

Not only continual prayer but continual praise. "In everything by prayer and supplication with thanksgiving." Our prayers should be mingled with thanksgiving for many reasons.

The first practical reason: prayer will be sure to cause depression if you do not mingle it with thanksgiving. In prayer you may get too much occupied with self; you turn to search out all your needs and they are so many you will be in danger of getting anxious. Here is the cure for it: the apostle says, "Always pray with thanksgiving." Begin your prayer with worship and thanksgiving.

Another reason for thanksgiving: it pleases God. It will draw Him to you. Begin your prayer with praise. It will light up your heart. It will make you rejoice in God, and joy gives new power in prayer. Begin your prayer with praise. It will give wings to your faith. When you think of what God has done and what God has promised to do, praise Him for it! Thus, God will do more every day.

When you neglect to praise God, you rob Him of His glory and yourself of a precious privilege. When you hear of men converted, when you read a missionary letter showing blessing in His work, praise God for the work that is being done! When you hear of any good of a man, praise God for it! Take every opportunity for praising. You will find it ever leading you onward, ever upward. It gives a consciousness of God's goodness—of joy and trust in Him, ever mingling. Your heart will be established in the rest of faith.

4. Continual peace

"And the peace of God that passeth understanding shall keep you."
Who is there today that would like to have the peace of God—the
peace that passes all understanding? Who would desire it? Are
there any hearts here that say, "Would, God, that I could have it?"
Just think what a peace! What does it mean? It means this: not
only the peace that God gives. No, it is the peace of God Himself.

We read in the Hebrews that we must enter into the rest of God.
God says, "They are not entered into my rest" in Psalm 95[220], and
Hebrews tells us they had not been brought into the real rest, "But
we which have believed do enter into the rest of God"[221]—the rest
of knowing that God has finished His work; God has cared for
everything; I am a child of God. What a rest! The peace of God, that
great calm in which God ever dwells, can come down into my heart.

God gives His holy presence, and with that presence the sense of
His nearness and His love and His great peace. Don't separate the
peace of God from God Himself. God cannot give His peace the
way I take a piece of money out of my pocket and give it away from
me. Just as the light of the sun is always coming direct from the
sun and I must have the sun, then I can have the light; so it is with
the peace of God. I must have God, and when I have God then the
peace of God as an outflow will keep my heart. Who wants to have
the great peace of God? God is a being of infinite stillness and rest
and a peace passing all understanding. The soul that really
commits itself with every care to this God will have Him in His
perfect rest and peace. Take possession.

Beloved, you can have the presence of God every moment, and

---

[220] Psalm 95:11
[221] Hebrews 4:3

where the presence of God is, the great peace of God is. The great peace of God can be with you all day. How can I get it? "Be anxious for nothing." Trust God. Meet God and give up selfish desires into His bosom. With thanksgiving, praise and adore Him, and the peace of God shall come and fill your heart and life.

5. Continual safety

The fifth mark of the restful life is perfect safety. The word is a beautiful one. "The peace of God shall guard your heart and mind by Christ Jesus." Shall guard it. Shall keep it. You had that word last night, "Now unto Him who is able to keep."[222] How blessed to have heart and mind kept. I cannot keep them. The heart is always ready to wander and get discouraged, with its fears and perplexities. But in the great peace of God coming down to keep heart and mind, my whole nature may be kept through Christ Jesus.

Believers, I beseech you by the mercies of God to live this life of perfect rest. We have spoken to you about the Holy Spirit and His work, and Christ and His work revealed that He might bring us to God. And this text comes and says, "After you have brought yourself, bring every anxiety too, and every desire unto the living God, and leave it in His bosom." Be assured that as you reach out after God, He will send down the very peace of heaven to keep your heart and mind in Christ Jesus.

Dear Christians, is each one of us going to live in accordance with this blessed word? Ministers of the gospel who have got to preach to others, I quoted the word yesterday—I am going to quote it again because it made such a strong, deep impression in my heart—"The first duty of a clergy man is humbly to ask God that all that he wants done in those whom he teaches may first be fully and

---

[222] Jude 1:24

truly done in himself."[223]

Brother ministers, have we the great peace of God keeping our hearts and minds by Christ Jesus from morning to night, from Sunday to Saturday, in the pulpit, in the study, in the home, in society, in the street, in our whole life? If not, how can we preach it? God, give every servant of His in the ministry such an experience of the great peace of God ruling in his heart that he may be able to preach it in the power of the Holy Ghost! Ask God to do so.

And you workers, it is an easy thing to come and talk about the peace that has been made by the blood of Christ. We praise God for that peace, but there is something far deeper than that peace that was made by the blood of the cross; there is life ever kept in the peace with God. "Thou wilt keep him in perfect peace whose mind is stayed upon Thee."[224]

Christian workers, do pray. It is not the hurry, it is not the worry, it is not the study, not the running hither and thither, the much talking and much working that will have effect for eternity, but it is the great power of God. And God's power is revealed in the world, not in the earthquake so much, but in the still, small voice.[225]

Christian workers, students, come let us offer our hearts to God and ask Him very humbly, that His great peace may have perfect possession of us. And if we feel we have not got it and it won't come or that we have lost it, let us pray. Listen, "Be anxious for nothing." Do go with every anxiety direct to God, with praise, prayer and thanksgiving. Praise Him for what He is going to do, but be anxious for nothing. Let every foreboding anxiety drive you to God.

---

[223] Elsewhere Murray attributes this to William Law
[224] Isaiah 26:3
[225] 1 Kings 19:11-13

Christian workers, let the great peace of God enter your hearts today. Do walk as examples of men into whom God has poured His own peace, and let the humility and the lowliness and the meekness and the gentleness of Jesus Christ, the Lamb of God, be the mark of your life. God help us to that!

Amen.

Made in the USA
Columbia, SC
05 July 2022

62835936R00124